By
Alberto Bravo

and
Pepita Marín

we are knitters

knitspiration to take
anywhere and everywhere

Abrams, New York

Contents

Introduction

We were introduced to the DIY movement more than a decade ago. We were not knitters, crocheters, or makers then, but we most certainly are now. That's one of the many great things we love about crafting: Not everyone is born with these skills, but anyone can learn them. You have to practice, and with time you will only get better. And the best news is it's never too late to start learning. It doesn't matter if you're in school, or working, or living whatever version of the good life. Crafting has no age restrictions.

When learning a new skill, such as knitting or crochet, it's important to remember that it is a never-ending process. *But, wait!* We don't mean you will *never* finish a project (although sometimes you can have so many works-in-progress that it can feel like it may never end); we mean that there will always be new techniques, new stitches, new patterns, and new ways of doing the same thing. Always. Even advanced makers can learn new things. So just sit back and relax—you can even have a glass of wine if you like! If there is anything we makers have in common it's our love for wine (mostly red or rosé for us). Oh, and also our love for animals (mostly kittens and puppies—and sheep!) . . . anyway, like we were saying, crafting is something that takes time and patience.

Some of you may have been on the We Are Knitters journey with us for a while now, and some of you may have just joined. It doesn't matter.

What you will find in this book is for everyone. From the very first baby steps, explained in a very easy-to-follow way, to the more advanced and complicated techniques. We're ready to show you the stitches, tricks, and tips that will teach you the basics and then take you to the next level. Besides, as a maker, you enjoy a good challenge, right?

And what would a knitting book be without a collection of patterns? When compiling this book, it was so hard to determine which patterns to include. We definitely wanted to have some WAK classics (like the Downtown Snood, Martina Cardigan, and Bryant Scarf) but we also wanted some new ones (like the Encina Scarf, Olmo Headband, and Pino Pillow) that fit different styles at different levels for different tastes, to keep things exciting. In the end, we came up with what we think is a perfect assortment: some new, some old, but all for you. We really hope you like them. We certainly do.

After we decided on the right patterns for this book, we took our work on the road. Each piece was shot in a different city in America, Europe, and Africa. Each one has a special place in our hearts for some reason or another, and we cannot deny that we had a blast traveling to all of those amazing places! So much so that we also included tips about the local weather, what we love to eat while we're there, and, *of course*, our favorite places to knit! These three things will be your essentials during any trip to these locations (OK, OK, they're *some* of your essentials).

So whether you prefer to knit at home, or you're ready to grab your passport and a map and hit the road, this is the book for you. Now it's time to pick up your needles and a beautiful skein of yarn, and make as much as you can with all of this #knitspiration. Enjoy the ride!

About This Book

As with all of our patterns, each project in this book has a particular style and skill level associated with it. Whether you're a novice knitter or can knit circles around your own grandma, there's something here for everyone (and we believe by the time you are done reading, everything will be doable for you).

Styles

When designing new styles, we're usually inspired by what we see on the streets. Fashion magazines, blogs, Pinterest, and Instagram are good sources, too. It's kind of a guilty pleasure to imagine all of the pieces that we would love to make, even though we know there is not enough time to make them all! We're pretty sure you get where we're coming from.

Our designs are mostly created for women, although we have quite a few patterns that can be worn by anyone. We also love creating patterns for home decor and, *of course*, designs for babies and kids. The good thing about makers is that with a pair of needles or a hook, some yarn, and a bit of creativity, we can make just about anything. The possibilities are endless!

The pieces in this book were chosen for their style, and we hope they are instructional and inspirational when thinking about what you might make next.

Levels

First time with a pair of needles in your hands? Don't panic! The great thing about knitting it is that you'll see results from the very beginning. All you have to do is relax, inhale, exhale, and have a little bit of patience. After all, at some point all knitters were not knitters, you know? In fact, you should have seen the very first collection we launched. Yikes! Super easy patterns, mostly squares, yet we were super proud because we were able to actually make them. Ahh, that feeling . . .

As with most things in life, time and practice will only make you better. That's why, bit by bit, we started to design more complicated patterns and styles that could be a challenge for the more experienced knitters, too. As a result of all this, nowadays we have four different levels: beginner, easy, intermediate, and advanced.

we are knitters

BEGINNER

Simple shapes and basic stitches. If you've never picked up a pair of needles, this is your starting level. These patterns are the perfect place to begin.

The types of garments we recommend you knit as a beginner are snoods, scarves, and simple beanies.

The most popular stitches in beginner patterns are garter, stockinette, and rib stitch.

EASY

Our most popular patterns are easy level, and they can be a great challenge for beginners, too!

The types of garments that you can knit at the easy level are snoods, scarves, beanies, simple sweaters (no increases or decreases—more on this later), and blankets.

Popular stitches include garter, stockinette, rib, seed, moss, and simple knit and purl combinations. The possibilities are almost endless!

INTERMEDIATE

When you are at the intermediate level, you can knit very sophisticated garments (we've always loved that word to describe knitting!).

Popular stitches include cross stitch, cables, twists, two-colored seed stitch, simple jacquard, simple lace stitches, bobbles, and loops.

ADVANCED

As an experienced knitter, there are no boundaries for you. You're what we call a *pro*. You can also create your own patterns at this point, we imagine!

Popular advanced stitches include complex lace stitches and advanced jacquard.

Makers Gonna Make

What is creativity without the necessary tools to create? Or more importantly, what is creativity if you don't know the basics and the technique you are about to practice? You got it: nothing. In this chapter we'll tell you more about the materials we like to use when knitting or crocheting—that is, our favorite types of yarn, how you can take care of them, and the needles you'll need—along with knitting basics and techniques, and the different effects you can create. Isn't it exciting? We think so, too!

The Yarn

At WAK, everything we choose is natural, and we are committed to making the world a greener place. But how? The answer is simple: Our wool is 100 percent sheep and alpaca, without an ounce of acrylic fiber. As an unnatural fiber, acrylic is possibly one of the environment's most dangerous silent enemies. According to a study Plymouth University (UK) did during a twelve-month period, acrylic fibers released 730,000 tiny synthetic particles per wash. Where do all these particles go? You guessed it: oceans. We cannot see them, we cannot feel them, but shorelines around the world are all covered with these microfibers, mostly made of acrylic and nylon. And that's not good for the ocean, the planet, or for us. WAK is committed to doing our part to curb habits and contributions that negatively impact our world, and we're committed to helping you do the same.

100% Peruvian Wool and Pima Cotton

Our wool comes from the high Andes in South America. It is obtained from sheep (Corriedale and Merino, to be exact) that are raised at an altitude of 6,500 feet (2,000 m) above sea level. Alpacas are raised a bit higher, living up to 14,000 feet (4,300 m) above sea level.

We also carry Pima cotton. Along with Egyptian cotton, Pima cotton is considered to be one of the finest in the world. Sourced from Peru, this type of cotton is softer and stronger than other types of cotton. But why? Because the fibers that compose it are 50 percent longer than those of standard cotton. Nowadays it is

only grown in Peru, Australia, and the United States. To put this into perspective: only about 3 percent of the cotton grown in the United States is Pima cotton. This is one of the main reasons it is so valuable and special.

Happy Animals

When we were first looking for wool suppliers, we only had two requirements: It needed to be top quality yarn, and it had to be ethically sourced. Everyone knows that Peruvian wool is one of the best in the world. But what about the animals? And what about the people that work with these animals? Visiting their facilities and farms in the highlands of Peru was a personal highlight for us: to realize that our work was going to help and influence all these local communities that were looking after sheep and alpacas was probably one of the proudest moments in our lives.

In the Peruvian Andes, our sheep and alpacas live in optimal conditions, in a natural environment, which directly impacts the quality of the wool.

Sometimes these animals and local families live so high up that conditions are quite hard. It's cold most of the time, and there is much less oxygen in the air than what most of us are used to (we have visited the area a few times over the years and believe us when we tell you that you feel tired most of the time and have a minor headache 24/7). It is very common for each local family to take care of a group of flocks, and

not surprisingly, women are the ones in charge of the animals' care. They are called *pastoras* or *alpaqueñas,* and they are incredible, strong, hardworking women.

Animals in the area can live up to twelve years, although their wool is only used during their first eight years. Alpacas only give birth once per year, and they are sheared only once per season, making their fiber a very valuable material. There are different types of sheep (Merino, Corriedale, Leicester, and Hampshire, to name a few) but all of them are sheared just once per year, normally during the springtime. Shearing is an important part of caring for sheep and alpacas and ensuring that they live healthy lives. Otherwise the weight of this wool could damage their legs—a single sheep can grow between eight and eleven pounds of wool each year. Can you imagine carrying that weight on your back all the time? Day and night? We can't either.

The Yarn Process

This is the process we use to obtain our 100 percent wool yarn.

1.
SHEARING THE ANIMALS
At the end of winter, sheep and alpacas no longer need their natural protection, and in the spring shearers shave their wool.

The animals are left cooler for the heat of the summer, and, don't worry, the animals live in good conditions and do not suffer at any time. Part of our team has visited the Highlands to check and verify that everything is done properly and to our high standards.

2.
WASHING THE WOOL
The sheared wool is washed in hot water and a sanitizing solution to remove dirt and impurities.

we are knitters

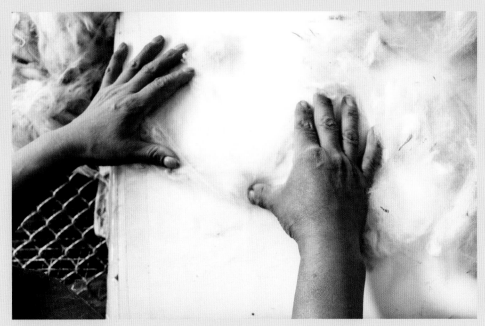

3 — Carding the Wool

3.
CARDING THE WOOL
Carding consists of gently picking and carefully pulling the pieces of fleece into fibers. The wool is carded and then combed.

4.
SPINNING THE WOOL
The wool fibers are mixed and twisted to the desired thickness. Usually a spindle or spinning wheel is used.

5.
DYEING THE YARN
The dye is poured into a pot with boiling water. The yarn is placed in the pot and left to absorb the color. Our yarns naturally tend to be a purer shade of white, so they can be dyed a wide range of colors. Some of the colors we use cannot be found in nature, so some of the dyes are not natural, but they are still biodegradable.

6.
TWISTING/PLYING THE YARN
The yarn is twisted once again, to give it the final touch, and that's it! We now have a skein of wool in our chosen color.

5 — Dyeing the Yarn

Characteristics of the Wool

When it comes to choosing the perfect yarn for your project, there are a few things you will need to keep in mind. It doesn't matter if you are a beginner or a super knitter, it doesn't matter the project or its use, you must follow the rules. There is no escape. Sorry—not sorry.

First, take into account the thickness of the yarn. The thicker it is, the faster you will move along in your project. This is because there will be fewer stitches and rows to work on. If you are a beginner, we recommend starting with a big, chunky wool. This way you will see results quickly and will feel encouraged to continue! Another reason thick yarn is better for beginners is because it is a lot easier to see mistakes and fix errors. All makers know how frustrating it is to undo work, but it's part of the larger process.

Once you get started using a very thick yarn, little by little you can start using thinner materials. This will enable you to create more detail and produce more elaborate techniques, like lace, cables, and jacquard, for example. Experiment with all of these and more!

Then there is the seasonality of the project. For autumn and winter, we recommend fibers such as wool or baby alpaca because of their warmth and great thermal insulation. Among these fibers, you can choose thicker or thinner yarns—thick ones are very warm but create a bulkier final piece, and thinner yarns insulate less but they are also less heavy, less bulky, and fit much closer to the body. For summer, we suggest fibers such as bamboo, linen, or cotton, because they are very light, fresh, and more pleasant when in direct contact with the skin.

20

Lastly think about how often you'll use the garment. All-natural fibers are delicate; therefore, we wouldn't recommend you wash them with chemicals or in a machine. If you are into natural wool but plan to wear the garment more regularly, we would suggest using fibers with a superwash treatment. This type of yarn is more resistant to pilling and is easier to wash. You can find more details about this procedure in the wool care section (see page 22).

Caring for WAK Wool and Cotton

Now that you've made your WAK piece, we want you to wear it with pride for a long, long, looong time. Taking caring of your handmade clothes is easy; you just need to follow a few tips to keep them looking brand new.

DO Wash by Hand

Natural materials are delicate and must be treated with care. Therefore, we advise you to wash your 100 percent wool or cotton garments by hand. Sorry, *c'est la vie*.

Begin by filling a bowl with cold water mixed with a little bit of mild soap. Mild soap is less abrasive, and you can find many different types suitable for wool. Leave your garment to soak for a few minutes, then rinse it gently to remove the soap residue.

DO NOT Wring the Garment

Never twist or rub the garment! Like never, ever. Not even while washing it or when drying it out. Just don't. Wringing the garment can cause it to become deformed, and rubbing it can give it an aged look. Ideally, roll the garment up in a towel to absorb excess water.

DO Lay Flat to Dry

How you dry your garments is just as important as how you wash them. Lay the garment on a flat, horizontal surface and keep it out of direct sunlight. This will prevent it from deforming from the weight of water and prevent the colors from being damaged by the sun.

DO NOT Use a Dryer

The dryer is not a friend to wool and cotton fabrics, and is, in fact, their biggest enemy! When exposed to high temperatures, natural fibers can shrink or felt and are likely to pill, giving an ugly and aged appearance to your clothes. Just keep them out of the dryer.

DO NOT Iron

If you follow the advice above, you will not need to iron your knit piece. Both wool and cotton will shrink a bit if exposed to the hot plate of an iron. As an alternative, you can use a lot of steam—avoid pressing the iron directly onto the garment—or set the iron at a low temperature and place a piece of cloth in between the iron and your knit piece. This will prevent it from becoming misshapen or shiny.

DO NOT Hang the Garment

Once they are cleaned and dry, do not hang your garments on a hanger. Keep them folded and without much weight on them so they do not become misshapen or lose their fluffiness.

SUPERWASH FIBERS

Although we always recommend washing all knitwear by hand, superwash fibers can be machine-washed. This type of yarn has undergone a special treatment that allows you to wash your projects in the machine without the concern of ruining the garment. These fibers are a good option if you're thinking about making something for babies/kids, or you're planning to wear the piece quite a lot. Just choose a delicate cycle, use mild soap, let your garment dry flat, and you'll see great results! (FYI: Among all WAK fibers, only Meriwool is superwash.)

The Tools

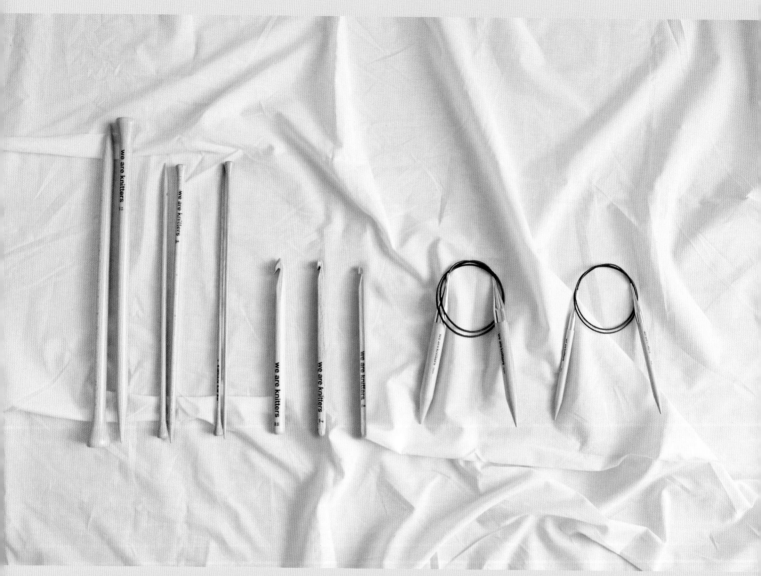

WAK needles and hooks.

we are knitters

Needles are to a knitter what a wand is to a magician: They are everything! Needles are the tools with which we work for many hours. Therefore, it's very important that they are high quality, appropriate for the fiber you're using, and very comfortable.

At WAK, we are partial to our beechwood needles. We work with Spanish artisans to make them one by one. But the beechwood we like to use is not just any wood! We source ours from certified forests. Never heard of that? Forest certification ensures sustainable forest management, supported by the main international environmental organizations. To obtain this certification, forests must meet high standards in conservation of biodiversity, soil protection, water quality, and even worker safety. In short, buying from certified forests means that we have a lower impact on the environment and a more responsible use of resources. Stay green, friends!

1. They have no nickel, so they're not a concern for those with skin allergies.
2. Wooden needles have a warm and special touch.
3. The rounded tip is great because the needles won't damage your yarn while you knit your garment.
4. They are lightweight.
5. They don't slip through your fingers, which is great for beginners who don't need added distractions.
6. You can knit with them almost everywhere, even on planes.
7. The clicking is softer and more melodic.

FUN FACT: This book is made from paper from certified forests!

Knitting Basics — Cast On

Casting on is the first thing you need to learn in order to knit your project. It's the foundation of all knitting.

To start, you need a strand of yarn three times longer than the piece you're casting on for.
　That is, if your garment is 8" (20.5 cm) long, use a strand 24" (61 cm) long.

1.
Make a slipknot as shown.

2.
Insert a needle into the slipknot and adjust the knot on the needle. Don't make it too tight, or it will be hard to work with it. With your left hand, hold the yarn coming from the ball, and with your right hand, hold the other strand.

we are knitters

3.
With your left hand, make a loop with the yarn and put it on the needle.

4.
Wrap the yarn with your right hand around the needle, going over the needle from left to right.

5.
Pull the loop in your left hand over the wrap and off the needle. You just made the second stitch. Pull both strands lightly to adjust it to the needle.

6.
Repeat steps 3–5 until you have the desired number of stitches.

Knitting Basics — Knit Stitch

The first stitch you will learn how to make is the knit stitch, since it's the base for all the other stitches.

we are knitters

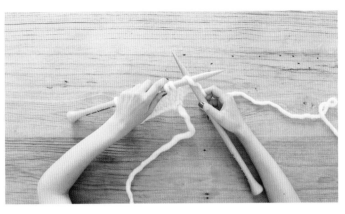

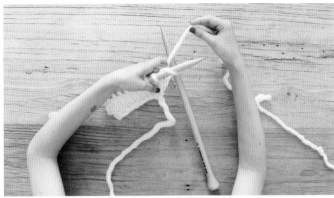

1.

With your left hand, hold the needle with the stitches. With the yarn behind the needle, insert the right-hand needle into the center of the first stitch, as shown.

2.

Wrap the yarn around behind the right-hand needle from right to left, then over the top of the right-hand needle from left to right, creating a loop on the needle.

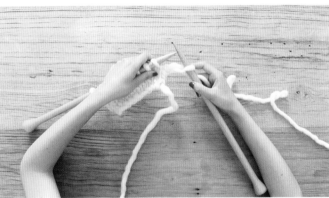

3.

Gently take the tip of the right-hand needle under the left-hand needle toward you, pulling the new loop through the original stitch on the left-hand needle.

4.

Slide the stitch off the left-hand needle.

5.

Repeat steps 1–4 to knit.

Knitting Basics — Purl Stitch

This is the next stitch you must learn to make. Once you master the knit and purl stitches, you can combine them to create designs and textures.

we are knitters

1.
With your left hand, hold the needle with the stitches. With the yarn in front of the needle, insert the right-hand needle into the center of the first stitch, making it pass in front of the left-hand needle, as shown.

2.
With your right hand, wrap the yarn over the top of the right-hand needle and back around to the front, creating a loop on the needle.

3.
Gently take the tip of the right-hand needle under the left-hand needle to the back, pulling the new loop through the original stitch on the left-hand needle.

4.
Slide the stitch off the left-hand needle.

5.
Repeat steps 1–4 to purl.

makers gonna make — knitting basics

Knitting Basics — Bind Off

Once you have finished your project, you will need to bind off the stitches in order to remove your knitted piece from the needle.

1.
Start by slipping the first stitch to the right-hand needle without working it.

2.
Knit the second stitch. Then, insert the tip of the left-hand needle into the front of the first stitch on the right-hand needle (the right-most stitch), and draw that stitch over the second stitch and off the needle. There will only be one stitch remaining on the right-hand needle. You have now bound off one stitch.

we are knitters

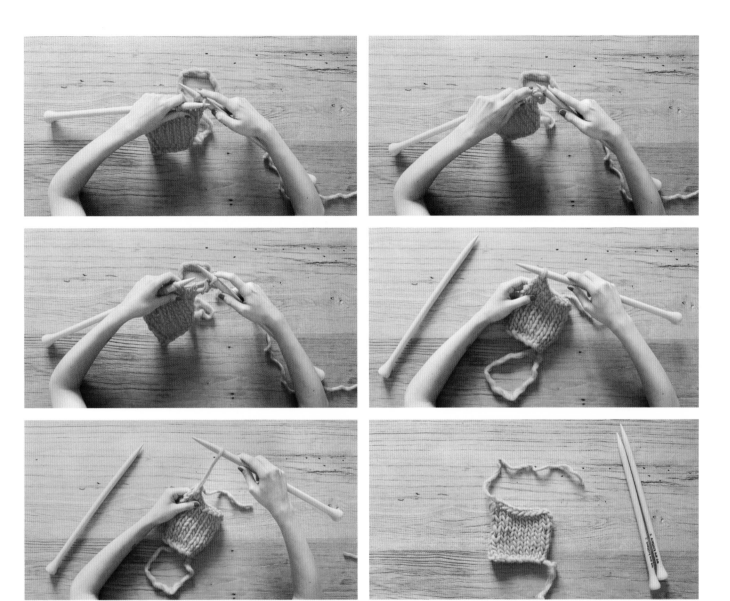

3.
Repeat from step 2 until you have bound off the desired number of stitches.

4.
When you reach the last stitch, cut the yarn leaving an 8" (20.5 cm) tail and pull the tail through the last loop on your needle. Thread the tail onto a tapestry needle and, with the wrong side of the work facing you, run the tail through the back of a few inches of stitches to hide the tail, being careful not to let the tail show on the right side. Trim the tail close to the work.

Knitting Basics — Slip Stitch

Sometimes you will have to slip a stitch without knitting or purling it. These are the easy steps you need to follow.

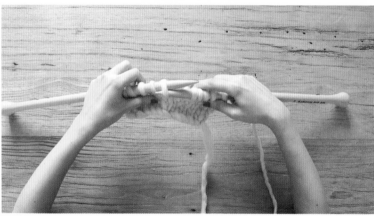

1.

Insert the right-hand needle into the stitch you want to slip, as if you were going to purl it.

2.

Slip it to the right-hand needle without working it.

This technique is often used at the beginning of a row to create a nice, clean edge on your project.

we are knitters

Basic Stitches — Garter Stitch

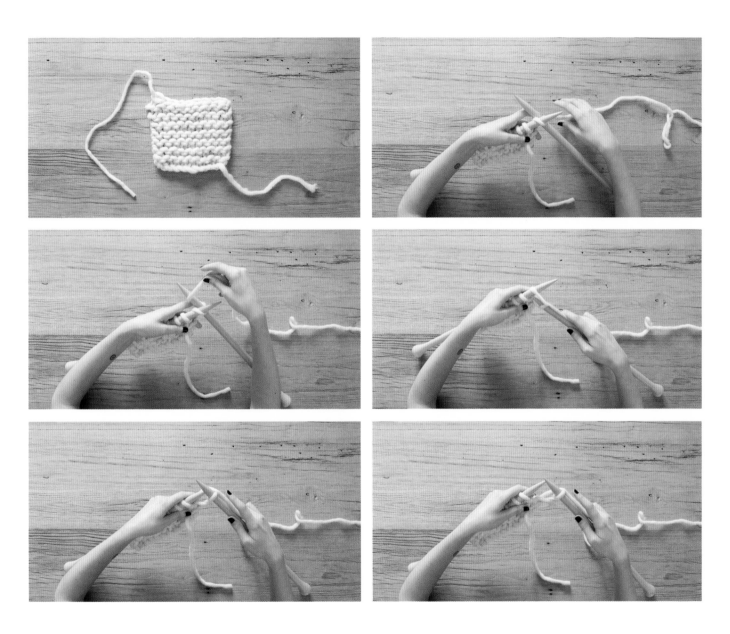

Garter stitch is the most basic and easy stitch in knitting.

1.

Cast on any number of stitches.

2.

Knit all stitches and all rows until you reach the desired length.

Basic Stitches — Stockinette Stitch

Stockinette stitch is the most
common stitch used in garments.

1.
Cast on any number of stitches
Row 1: Knit all stitches.

Row 2: Purl all stitches.

2.
Repeat rows 1 and 2 until you reach the desired length.

NOTE: There is a variation of this called reverse stockinette stitch where odd rows are purled and even rows are knitted.

Basic Stitches — 1x1 Rib Stitch

Rib stitch is normally used to give elastic finishing to necklines, cuffs, and bottoms.

1.
Cast on an even number of stitches.
Row 1: *Knit 1 stitch, purl 1 stitch*.
Repeat from * to * until the end of the row.**

NOTE: When, in the same row, you work a knit stitch followed by a purl stitch (or vice versa), you have to change the position of your working yarn. Place the working yarn in front of your work to make a purl stitch and place the working yarn in back of your work to make a knit stitch.

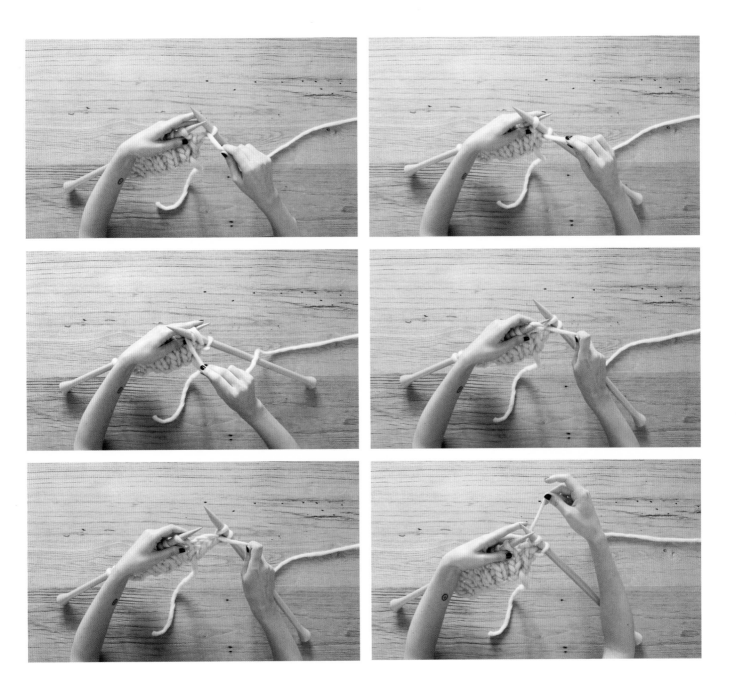

2.
Repeat row 1 until you reach the
desired length.

Basic Stitches — Seed Stitch

Seed stitch is usually used to knit textured garments due to its visual effect.

1.
Cast on an odd number of stitches.
Row 1: *Knit 1 stitch, purl 1 stitch*.
Repeat from * to * until the end of the row.

2.
Repeat row 1 until you reach the desired length.

we are knitters

makers gonna make — knitting basics

Changing Yarn — Classic Method

This technique is used to join two balls of yarn, if the one you are using runs out, or if you want to change to a new color in your project.

1.
When the yarn is about to run out, stop working with it at the end of the row. It's important that the strand is at the end of the row to better hide the join. Take the new yarn and hold it with your left hand behind the project.

2.
Work the next row as usual, using the new ball of yarn.

3.
When you are done with the row, tie a little knot to join both yarn strands. After finishing the project, weave in each end into its corresponding color section.

we are knitters

— Felting Method

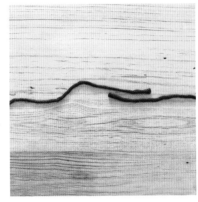

This is our favorite technique to join 100 percent wool yarn; it cannot be used for superwash wool or cotton, neither of which can be felted.

There are two ways to perform this technique.

A.
With a carding needle: If you have a carding needle, it's very easy. Place the strand from the finished ball next to the strand from the new ball, and with the needle, felt one strand together with the other by poking the carding needle through both strands at the same time until they are firmly joined together into one strand.

B.
Without a carding needle: If you don't have a carding needle, don't worry. Dampen both strands with warm water. Rub the strands against each other with your hands. The strands will become permanently joined.

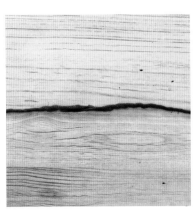

Double-Stranded Knitting

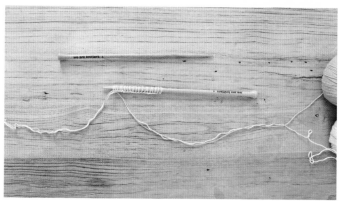

Now that you know the basic techniques, why don't we play with texture? Knitting a fabric has endless possibilities: Sometimes that can mean using larger- or smaller-sized needles than recommended for that yarn to get a different texture or effect, and sometimes that can mean knitting with two strands at once. Here, we'll show you how to work with two strands at the same time. This can be used to give your project a marled or multicolor look or to increase the thickness of the fabric.

1.
Grab the tail from the ball of your first color and the tail from the ball of your second color.

2.
Hold them together as if they were one strand, making sure that when you knit or purl into a stitch that you don't separate the strands.

3.
Work like this for as many rows as you want.

You may also try working some sections with a double strand and some with a single strand. The single-strand sections will have a looser fabric than the double-strand sections if you use the same needles throughout.

Increasing Stitches —

Increases are used to add more stitches to the needle. This is useful for shaping sleeves or the side edges of garments. Shown here using knit stitch.

1.

Insert your right-hand needle from front to back under the strand between the last stitch on the

right-hand needle and the first stitch on the left-hand needle.

2.

Place the strand on the left-hand needle.

3.

Knit into the back of the strand, creating a new stitch while twisting the stitch—this prevents a hole being created in the fabric.

we are knitters

Yarnover Increases

Yarnovers are used to make a new stitch while deliberately creating a hole in the project. They are most often combined with one or more decreases (see Decreasing Stitches, page 48) to create lace.

1.
Bring the yarn under the right-hand needle to the front, then over the needle to the back.

2.
Knit the next stitch.

3.
On the next row (the purl side), you will purl that strand as if it were a regular stitch. This will result in an increased stitch and an intentional small hole in your project.

Decreasing Stitches — Knit 2 Together

Decreases are used to subtract stitches in order to shape things like necklines, armholes, and waistlines. They are also used to make ornamental stitches like eyelets or netted stitches.

This is the easiest technique for decreasing stitches. It's made by knitting two stitches at the same time, as if they were one.

1.
Insert the right-hand needle into the next two stitches as if they are one.

2.
Knit them together as if they were only one stitch.

The end result is similar to a regular knit stitch, but it leans slightly to the right. If you want a left-leaning decrease, keep reading, and we'll show you how to make one.

we are knitters

— Purl 2 Together

Purl 2 together is similar to knit 2 together, except that it is worked over two purl stitches instead of two knit stitches.

1.
Insert the right-hand needle into the front of the next two stitches as if they are one.

2.
Purl them together as if they were only one stitch.

When you look at this decrease from the knit side of the fabric, it leans slightly to the right.

— Slip, Knit, Pass Over

This is a mirror decrease for the knit 2 together decrease, since it leans slightly to the left when it is completed. Working slip, knit, pass over, and knit 2 together on opposite edges of your project will make the edges symmetrical.

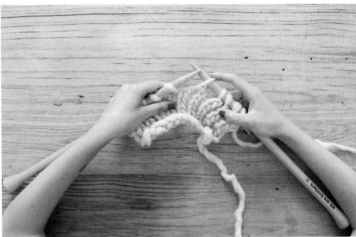

1.
Slip 1 stitch as if you were going to knit it.

2.
Knit the next stitch.

3.
Using the left-hand needle, pass
the slipped stitch over the knit
stitch and off the right-hand needle.

Working Cables

Along with lace, cables are one of the most fun techniques in knitting. Once you learn the basics, you'll be able to play with the width of a cable, starting with small cables and moving on to wider cables. But first, let's start with a very basic one. To begin, you'll need some knit stitches for the cable, and some stitches on either side of the cable, which are usually purled.

For this example, we have cast on 14 stitches, distributed as follows: 4 purl stitches at each side and 6 knit stitches in the middle for the cable.

1.
Slip the number of stitches specified in the pattern (in this case, 3 stitches) to a cable needle and leave them on hold in front or back of your project, as indicated in the pattern (in this case, in back).

2.
Work the next stitches as indicated by the pattern (in this case, knit 3).

we are knitters

3.
Return the stitches that you had on hold in the cable needle to the left-hand needle and knit or purl the stitches from the cable needle (in this case, knit them).

You have now made your first cable. Make sure to work an odd number of rows after each cable row so that the next cable row is worked on the same side of the work as the previous one.

Work just a few rows between cables for a compact cable, or more rows for an elongated cable.

Work the Stitches as They Appear

Working the stitches as they appear is a very common term used in the patterns. This means knit the knit stitches, and purl the purl stitches.

1.
Knit the knit stitches.

2.
Purl the purl stitches.

Cast on Stitches at the Beginning of a Row (Knitted Cast-On)

Casting on stitches at the beginning of a row is used to add 2 or more stitches and shape sleeves and necklines.

1.
When you have to cast on stitches at the beginning of a row, insert the right-hand needle into the first

stitch and wrap the yarn around the needle as if you were going to knit the stitch. Pull through to create

a new stitch on the right-hand needle.

2.
Insert the tip of the left-hand needle into the front of the new stitch on the right-hand needle from right to left and transfer it to the left-hand needle.

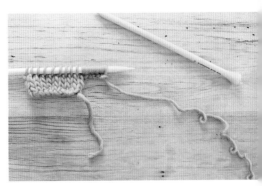

3.
You have cast on one stitch. Repeat this cast-on as many times as indicated in the pattern. After casting on the number of stitches called for, work them as indicated in the pattern.

Mattress Stitch

The mattress stitch is used to seam and connect the finished pieces; this technique will give your garments a very neat finishing.

1.
Cut a length of the same yarn you used for your project and thread a tapestry needle with it.

2.
Put both pieces that you are sewing on a flat surface with the right side facing you.

3.
Introduce the tapestry needle into the strand of yarn between the first stitch and the second stitch of the first row from the right piece.

4.

Then introduce the tapestry needle into the strand of yarn between the first stitch and the second stitch of the first row from the left piece.

5.

Repeat steps 3 and 4 to sew the rest of the rows.

6.

Once you are done sewing both pieces, pull the yarn to tighten the seam.

Pick Up and Knit

This technique is used to finish necklines and sleeves.

1.
Insert the knitting needle into the first stitch of the first row.

we are knitters

2.
Wrap the yarn around your needle
and pull the needle with the yarn
through this first stitch. You will
have picked up the first stitch.

3.
Insert the needle into the first stitch
of the second row, wrap the yarn
around the needle and pull the
needle with the yarn through the
stitch. You will have 2 stitches on
your needle.

4.
Continue picking up the first stitch
of every row.

Gauge

Even if two knitters were to knit following exactly the same instructions, using the same needles and yarn, their pieces would not look exactly the same. Strange, isn't it? The size of a piece is not only influenced by the yarn and needle size, but also by the gauge at which the knitter knits. The amount of pressure that the knitter exerts on the yarn when knitting directly affects their gauge.

we are knitters

It is essential to work up a gauge swatch before beginning a project. That way we can find out if our knitting is too tight or too loose, and we can adjust the needle size to give us the gauge that we need. To make a gauge swatch, simply work a square measuring 8 x 8" (20.5 x 20.5 cm) using the stitch pattern and needle size indicated in the pattern. Doing a bigger sample will make it easier to measure 4 x 4" (10 x 10 cm) of stitches and rows.

1.
Once bound off, hand-wash the swatch and lay it flat to dry completely. To measure the stitches in one row, place a pin vertically between two stitches, 1" (2.5 cm) or so in from one edge.

2.
Lay a flat ruler below the pin, along the base of one horizontal line of stitches, then place a second pin 4" (10 cm) from the first pin, noting that the second pin might be one quarter or one half of the way through a stitch.

NOTE: Avoid using measuring tapes, as these can stretch and yield inaccurate measurements.

3.

Now you have to count all the little "V"s that form the stitches. You can do that with the help of a knitting needle so that you don't lose count.

4.

In the picture, we have highlighted every stitch so that it is easier for you to count them. Don't forget to include any partial stitch in your stitch count. According to our swatch, we have 6 stitches in 4" (10 cm).

5.

Use the same method to measure the rows that you have in 4" (10 cm), highlighting the stitches vertically.

Again, every "V" indicates a row. In our swatch, we have 11 rows.

Can you see how easy it all is? Now, you should compare your sample with the pattern gauge. If the result is the same, you can start your project! But if it's not the same, you have a few options:

- You can increase or decrease the size of your needles and swatch the pattern again until your gauge matches the gauge in the pattern. This is the preferred option, since it allows you to relax and knit naturally, knowing your gauge is correct.
- You can knit using more or less tension on the yarn. This will require you to pay close attention to your stitches as you're knitting.
- You can work the project using your gauge rather than the gauge called for in the pattern. You will need to adjust the number of stitches that you cast on in order to obtain the same measurements indicated in the pattern. We only recommend this option for very experienced knitters, because it will require numerous other changes to the pattern in order to make it work correctly.

We understand that it can be annoying to always knit a swatch before you start knitting, but it is the best way to ensure that you achieve the results you are looking for!

Mixing Yarns and Creating Effects

As makers, we love different textures, don't we? It's so satisfying to see and feel something new in each project. However, sometimes the yarn we're using doesn't provide the texture we want, so we have to turn to different techniques and tricks.

Usually combining fibers is a great solution for creating different textures. For example, combining the same fiber in two different colors creates a marled shade. This technique is perfect when knitting sweaters without textured stitch patterns, such as ones made in garter stitch or stockinette stitch.

An example of this technique would be the Tuareg Sweater (page 80). In this design, a very thick wool is mixed with two different shades of a much thinner cotton yarn. In addition to rigidity, cotton gives a beautiful edge to the final piece, don't you think?

we are knitters

Another technique is using different needle sizes with the same yarn, which will result in different textures or densities. For example, knitting with needles much larger than the ones recommended lightens the fabric, adds drape, gives a woven appearance, and creates a more transparent fabric. Using smaller needles than what's recommended adds weight and rigidity to the project.

We also suggest mixing yarns with different weights: Start by knitting a few rows of your project with a thinner yarn than what's called for in the project, then knit with the recommended one. Change again (or not) as many times as you want! This will give a lacy look in the parts you used the thinner yarn. You can see an example of this technique in the Tribunal Cardigan (page 72).

When mixing yarns, the possibilities are endless because you can play with different colors, materials, and weights. The most important thing is to try whatever comes to mind and look for balance and harmony.

The Patterns

"Better to see something once than hear about it a thousand times."
—Unknown

Here you will find a grand total of fifteen different patterns (yaaas!): sweaters, cardis, scarves, beanies . . . even a headband! You'll also find a variety of stitches and techniques, from beginner knits to more advanced ones. Some of them might be easy, but others will definitely challenge your knitting skills—trust us.

Plus, you will see beautiful images of some of our favorite places in the world and get a taste of what it is like to visit, eat, and create there.

Now, fasten your seat belts and don't forget to bring your knitting needles. You might need them at your next destination!

Marrakech

WHERE TO KNIT
Le Jardin: An oasis in the middle of the medina. Full of plants, everything is green in this restaurant: the walls, the floor, the chairs, everything! Even turtles roam freely.

Nomad: A rooftop with beautiful views of the medina; it's the perfect place to have a drink and knit!

Le Jardin Majorelle: Yves Saint Laurent's shelter when in Marrakech. He lived here during long periods of his life. Now you can visit the peaceful gardens around the villa.

AVERAGE HIGH TEMPERATURES
Spring: 75.7°F (24.3°C)
Summer: 94.3°F (34.6°C)
Fall: 81.0°F (27.2°C)
Winter: 66.0°F (18.9°C)

RAINY SEASON
January and February

FAVORITE DISHES
Chicken tagine
Briouat

VEGGIE OPTIONS
Makouda
Vegetarian couscous

Don't ask us why, but we've always been intrigued by Morocco. Is it the terra-cotta color palette? Or maybe it's the country's sense of style, the maze that is the medina, or perhaps it's the food? Really, it's everything. Marrakech is a truly magical place.

To step into Marrakech is to be inspired. We went there a couple of years ago because we wanted to design a whole collection inspired by the city and oh-emm-gee! We were there for only a few days, but that was enough to take in the magic it had to offer. The architecture alone is simply stunning. You could stare at the ceiling of the most basic palace all day and you would still miss parts of it. So! Many! Details! Seriously.

In an attempt to translate all of this beauty into knitting patterns, we came up with the two pieces featured in this section: multi-fiber designs with different textures that give them that little extra something that Marrakech has.

we are knitters

Tribunal Cardigan

LEVEL
Intermediate

SIZES
Small [Medium, Large, X-Large]

FINISHED MEASUREMENTS
42 [45, 47, 50]" (106 [114, 120, 126] cm) bust

YARN
We Are Knitters The Petite Wool [100% Peruvian wool; 153 yards (140 meters)/100 grams]: 3 [3, 3, 3] balls Natural

We Are Knitters The Wool [100% Peruvian wool; 87 yards (80 meters)/200 grams]: 4 [4, 5, 5] balls Natural

NEEDLES
One 24" (60 cm) circular needle size US 19 (15 mm)
Change needle size if necessary to obtain correct gauge.

NOTIONS
Tapestry needle

GAUGE
6 sts and 9 rows = 4" (10 cm) in Stockinette stitch (see page 36)

● *Stitches*
○ *Rows*

patterns — marrakech

START KNITTING

BACK

Cast on 32 [34, 36, 38] stitches with The Petite Wool.

Work rows 1–66 [66, 68, 68] in Stockinette stitch following the alternating yarn pattern detailed below.

NOTE: Throughout the project, we will be alternating between The Petite Wool and The Wool.

Rows 1–4: The Petite Wool.
Rows 5–8: The Wool.
Rows 9 and 10: The Petite Wool.
Rows 11–14: The Wool.
Rows 15–18: The Petite Wool. Cut the yarn at the end of row 18.

NOTE: When you cut the yarn, make sure to leave a 3" (7.5-cm) yarn tail to weave in after you are finished knitting your garment.
Row 19: The Wool.
Rows 20–25: The Petite Wool.
Rows 26 and 27: The Wool.
Rows 28–31: The Petite Wool.
Rows 32–35: The Wool.

Rows 36 and 37: The Petite Wool. Cut the yarn at the end of row 37.
Row 38: The Wool.
Rows 39–44: The Petite Wool.
Rows 45–48: The Wool.
Rows 49–52: The Petite Wool. Cut the yarn at the end of row 52.
Row 53: The Wool.
Rows 54 and 55: The Petite Wool.
Rows 56 and 57: The Wool.
Rows 58–61: The Petite Wool.
Rows 62–66 [66, 68, 68]: The Wool.
Bind off all stitches.

FRONTS

Follow these instructions twice to make two fronts.

Cast on 15 [16, 17, 18] stitches with The Petite Wool.

Work rows 1–66 [66, 68, 68] the same as for the Back, following the same alternating yarn pattern.

Bind off all stitches.

SLEEVES

Follow these instructions twice to make two sleeves.

Cast on 12 [12, 14, 14] stitches with The Wool.

Work rows 1–10 with The Wool in 1x1 Rib stitch (see page 38).

Work rows 11–54 [54, 56, 56] in Stockinette stitch, increasing and working the alternating yarn as follows:

Row 11: Change to The Petite Wool. Knit 2 [1, 2, 1], increase 1, *knit 2 [2, 2, 2], increase 1*; repeat from * to * until there are 2 [1, 2, 1] stitch(es) left, knit to end. You will have a total of 17 [18, 20, 21] stitches.

Rows 12, 14, and 16: Purl all stitches with The Petite Wool.

Row 13: Knit 2 [1, 2, 1], increase 1; *knit 3 [3, 3, 3], increase 1*; repeat from * to * until there are 3 [2, 3, 2] stitches left, knit to end. You will have a total of 22 [24, 26, 28] stitches.

Row 15: Knit 2 [1, 2, 1], increase 1, *knit 4 [4, 4, 4], increase 1*; repeat from * to * until there are 4 [3, 4, 3] stitches left, knit to end. You will have a total of 27 [30, 32, 35] stitches.

Rows 17–52: Repeat rows 5–40 the same as for the Back, following the same alternating pattern.

Rows 53–54 [54, 56, 56]: Work Stockinette stitch with The Wool. Bind off all stitches.

SCHEMATICS

BACK

73 [73, 75, 75] *cm* | 29 [29, 30, 30] *in*
66 [66, 68, 68] ○

53 [57, 60, 63] *cm* | 21 [22½, 23½, 25] *in*
32 [34, 36, 38] ●

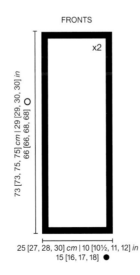

FRONTS

x2

73 [73, 75, 75] *cm* | 29 [29, 30, 30] *in*
66 [66, 68, 68] ○

25 [27, 28, 30] *cm* | 10 [10½, 11, 12] *in*
15 [16, 17, 18] ●

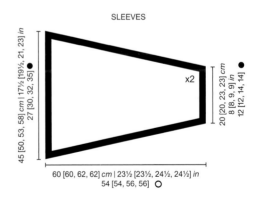

SLEEVES

x2

45 [50, 53, 58] *cm* | 17½ [19½, 21, 23] *in*
27 [30, 32, 35] ●

20 [20, 23, 23] *cm*
8 [8, 9, 9] *in*
12 [12, 14, 14] ●

60 [60, 62, 62] *cm* | 23½ [23½, 24½, 24½] *in*
54 [54, 56, 56] ○

1.

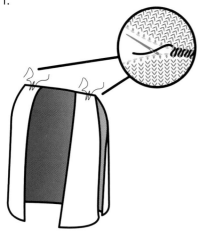

Thread a tapestry needle with the same Petite Wool that you used for your project and sew both of the shoulders together: Place the front and back with wrong sides together, lining up the shoulder seams. Sew 7 [8, 9, 10] stitches from each of the shoulders.

2.

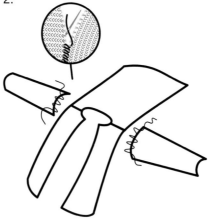

Sew a sleeve to the body of the cardigan, lining up the center of the sleeve with the shoulder seam. Repeat for the second sleeve.

3.

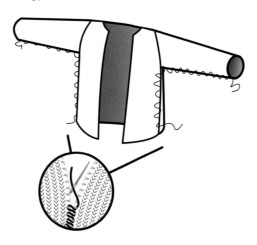

Next, sew the side seams and sleeve seams using the Mattress stitch (see page 56).

4.

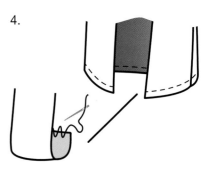

To hem the piece, fold the fronts and back in and under along row 4. Sew the hem in place on the wrong side of the cardigan, stitch by stitch, using the tapestry needle and The Petite Wool. Make a knot.

we are knitters

5.

Pull a length of about 30 feet (10 m) of The Wool and form a small ball. You will use this yarn to pick up stitches.

Using your needles and the small ball, pick up and knit 42 [42, 43, 43] stitches along the edge of the right front, starting at the bottom corner, as follows: *pick up and knit 2 stitches, skip 1*; repeat from * to * 19 [19, 20, 20] times, then pick up and knit 2 [2, 1, 1] stitches. Do not cut the yarn; leave it to be worked later. Slip all of the stitches that you picked up from the right-hand needle to the left-hand needle, so that the first stitch to be worked is the bottom front corner.

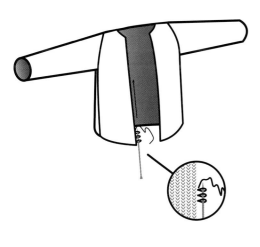

6.

We will finish the edge of the cardigan with I-cord. To do so, using yarn from the skein of The Wool, cast on 4 stitches at the beginning of the row.

A: Knit 3, slip 1, knit the next stitch from your left-hand needle, pass the slipped stitch over the stitch just knitted. Slip the stitches from the right-hand needle to the left-hand needle so that you can continue to work the same stitches without turning your work. This is called attached I-cord.

B: Repeat step A 41 [41, 42, 42] times, until you have bound off all of the picked-up stitches. You will have a total of 4 stitches on your needle.

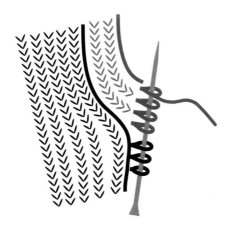

Continue around the neck as follows:

C: Work 3 rows of I-cord without joining it to your work. This means knit all of the stitches, slip them back to the left-hand needle and knit them again without turning your work.

D: Slip the 4 stitches that you have to the right-hand needle without working them. With the right-hand needle, pick up and knit 34 stitches from the neck (8 stitches from the right front, 18 stitches from the back, and 8 from the left front) using the yarn from the small ball that you separated earlier. Slip all of the stitches from the right-hand needle to the left-hand needle (34 stitches from the neck plus the 4 I-cord stitches), so that the first stitch to be worked is the corner of the I-cord.

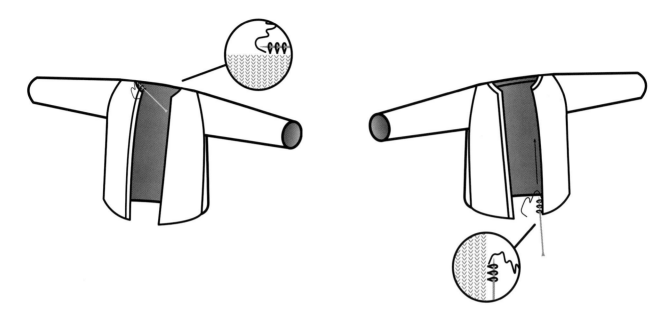

E: Using the yarn from the large skein, knit 3, slip 1, knit the next stitch from the left-hand needle, and pass the slipped stitch over the stitch you just knit. You have now joined the I-cord to your project again.

F: Continue working attached I-cord to the end of the neck stitches; you will have a total of 4 stitches.

G: Repeat step C for the corner of the neck of the left front.

H: Slip the 4 stitches to the right-hand needle and with the same needle pick up and knit 42 [42, 43, 43] stitches along the edge of the left front using the yarn from the small ball that you separated earlier, starting with the top corner, as follows: *pick up and knit 2 stitches, skip 1*; repeat from * to * 19 [19, 20, 20] times, pick up and knit 2 [2, 1, 1] stitches. Slip all of the stitches (the 42 [42, 43, 43] from the front plus 4 stitches from the I-cord) from the right-hand needle to the left-hand needle, so that the first stitch to be worked is the corner of the I-cord.

I: Using the yarn from the large skein repeat steps A and B.

J: Bind off all stitches.

7.
Weave in all ends.

Tuareg Sweater

LEVEL
Intermediate

SIZES
Small [Medium, Large, X-Large]

FINISHED MEASUREMENTS
37 (40, 44, 47)" [94 (102, 110, 120) cm] bust

YARN
We Are Knitters The Wool [100% Peruvian wool; 87 yards (80 meters)/200 grams]: 4 [4, 5, 5] balls Natural (A)

We Are Knitters The Pima Cotton [100% pima cotton; 232 yards (212 meters)/100 grams]: 1 [1, 2, 2] ball(s) each Black (B) and Salmon (C)

NEEDLES
One pair straight needles size US 19 (15 mm)
Change needle size if necessary to obtain correct gauge.

NOTIONS
Tapestry needle

GAUGE
9 sts and 17 rows = 4" (10 cm) in Tricolor Linen stitch (see page 82)

● *Stitches*
○ *Rows*

SCHEMATICS

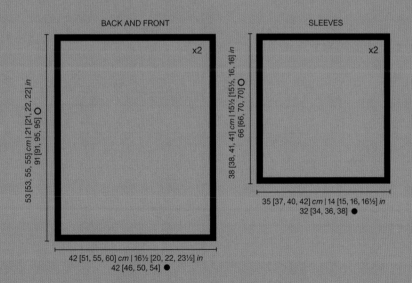

BACK AND FRONT

x2

53 [53, 55, 55] *cm* | 21 [21, 22, 22] *in*
91 [91, 95, 95] ○

42 [51, 55, 60] *cm* | 16½ [20, 22, 23½] *in*
42 [46, 50, 54] ●

SLEEVES

x2

38 [38, 41, 41] *cm* | 15½ [15½, 16, 16] *in*
66 [66, 70, 70] ○

35 [37, 40, 42] *cm* | 14 [15, 16, 16½] *in*
32 [34, 36, 38] ●

STITCH PATTERN
TRICOLOR LINEN STITCH

Row 1: With colors B and C held together, knit 1, *slip 1 with yarn in front, knit 1*; repeat from * to * until there is 1 stitch left, knit.

NOTE: When changing colors, do not cut the strand. Leave it behind the project, and grab it again when you need to.

Row 2: With colors B and C held together, knit 1, *slip 1 with yarn in back, purl 1*; repeat from * to * until there is 1 stitch left, knit.

Row 3: With color A alone, knit 1, *slip 1 with yarn in front, knit 1*; repeat from * to * until there is 1 stitch left, knit.

Row 4: With color A alone, knit 1, *slip 1 with yarn in back, purl 1*; repeat from * to * until there is 1 stitch left, knit.

Repeat rows 1 to 4 to work the Tricolor Linen stitch pattern.

START KNITTING

BACK AND FRONT
Follow these instructions twice to make the Back and the Front.
Cast on 42 [46, 50, 54] stitches with color A.
Work rows 1–90 [90, 94, 94] in Tricolor Linen stitch.
Row 91 [91, 95, 95]: With color A alone, knit 9 [11, 13, 15] and leave them on hold on a spare needle.
Bind off 24 stitches. Knit the remaining stitches and leave them on hold on a spare needle.

SLEEVES
Follow these instructions twice to make two sleeves.
Cast on 32 [34, 36, 38] stitches with color A.
Work rows 1–66 [66, 70, 70] in Tricolor Linen stitch.
Bind off all stitches with color A.

FINISHING

Kitchener stitch the shoulders together as follows. Place the sweater Front and Back wrong sides together.

1.
Thread a tapestry needle with one strand of color B and one of color C together and draw the strands through the first held stitch from the sweater Front as if you were going to purl it.

2.
Draw the strands through the first held stitch from the sweater Back as if you were going to knit it.

3.
Draw the strands through the first held stitch from the sweater Front as if you were going to knit it, and let the stitch drop from the needle.

4.
Draw the strands through the second stitch on the front needle as if you were going to purl it, leaving the stitch on the needle.

5.
Draw the strands through the first held stitch from the sweater Back as if you were going to purl, and let the stitch drop from the needle.

6.
Draw the strands through the second stitch on the back needle as if you were going to knit it, leaving the stitch on the needle.

Repeat steps 3–6 until all the stitches have been worked.

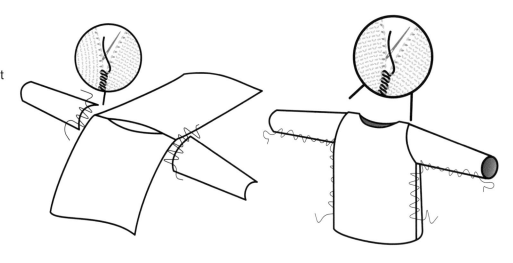

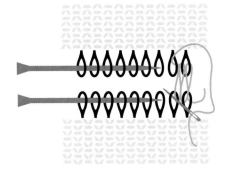

7.
Sew the sleeves to the body of the sweater, lining up the center of the sleeves with the shoulder seams.

8.
Next, sew the side seams and sleeve seams using Mattress stitch (see page 56).

9.
Weave in all ends.

Paris

WHERE TO KNIT
Jardin du Luxembourg:
These beautiful gardens
will make you feel as if you
are part of the Royal Court.
It's best to go during the
springtime when the flowers
are in full bloom.

Montmartre: Best known
because of Sacré-Coeur
and all the artists that
used to live here (including
Picasso, Renoir, and Van
Gogh), this neighborhood
still has that bohemian look
and feel that made it so
special a century ago.

Café de Flore: Located in
the 6th arrondissement, this
is one of the oldest cafés
in town. Its decoration and
menu will make you feel as
though you have traveled
back in time.

**AVERAGE HIGH
TEMPERATURES**
Spring: 59.0°F (15.0°C)
Summer: 74.5°F (23.6°C)
Fall: 59.9°F (15.5°C)
Winter: 45.1°F (7.3°C)

RAINY SEASON
April through May

FAVORITE DISHES
Magret de canard
Quiche Lorraine

VEGGIE OPTIONS
Ratatouille
Camembert cheese

Voulez-vous tricoter avec moi ce soir? Nope, this is not just our version of the famous line sung by Patti LaBelle, it is also what we like to imagine French makers ask each other during cold afternoons in Paris. Just maybe.

Paris is one of the most beautiful cities in the world and will always have a special place in WAK's heart. Along with Madrid, Paris was the first city that welcomed us and really gave us a chance when our business started to grow. Early on we noticed there were more and more French knitters using our kits, even though at that time our patterns were not available in French.

Like in most European countries in recent decades, where fewer and fewer people were picking up needles, knitting was *démodé* in France (we sound sooo French, right?) at the turn of the century. But with the new, slow-life revival, there are now tons of new knitters doing some really nice stuff. In fact, what makes you in vogue right now is to knit! The trendiest people in the City of Lights really enjoy making things with their own hands, whether it's knitting, crocheting, weaving, or macramé.

In this section we have some suggestions for pieces to knit while having a glass of wine in a beautiful café in Paris: a classic and timeless sweater, a simple but fun scarf, and a blanket that is easier to make than it looks. This section can only be described in three words: *ooh là là!*

we are knitters

patterns — paris

Classic Sweater

LEVEL
Easy

SIZES
Small [Medium, Large, X-Large]

FINISHED MEASUREMENTS
41 [43, 45, 47]" (104 [110, 114, 120] cm) bust

YARN
We Are Knitters The Petite Wool [100% Peruvian wool; 153 yards (140 meters)/100 grams]: 6 [6, 7, 7] balls Nude

NEEDLES
One pair straight needles size US 11 (8 mm) Change needle size if necessary to obtain correct gauge.

NOTIONS
Tapestry needle

GAUGE
13 sts and 22 rows = 4" (10 cm) in Garter stitch (see page 35)

● *Stitches*
○ *Rows*

SCHEMATICS

BACK AND FRONT

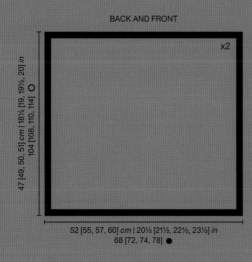

x2

47 [49, 50, 51] *cm* | 18½ [19, 19½, 20] *in*
104 [108, 110, 114] ○

52 [55, 57, 60] *cm* | 20½ [21½, 22½, 23½] *in*
68 [72, 74, 78] ●

SLEEVES

34 [35, 37, 38] *cm* | 13 [13½, 14½, 15] *in*
44 [46, 48, 50] ●

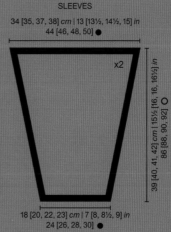

x2

39 [40, 41, 42] *cm* | 15½ [16, 16, 16½] *in*
86 [88, 90, 92] ○

18 [20, 22, 23] *cm* | 7 [8, 8½, 9] *in*
24 [26, 28, 30] ●

START KNITTING

BACK AND FRONT
Follow these instructions twice to make the Back and the Front.
Cast on 68 [72, 74, 78] stitches.
Work rows 1–6 in 1x1 Rib stitch (see page 38).
Work rows 7–104 [108, 110, 114] in Garter stitch.
Bind off all stitches.

SLEEVES
Follow these instructions twice to make two sleeves.
Cast on 24 [26, 28, 30] stitches.
Work rows 1–8 in 1x1 Rib stitch.
Rows 9–86 [88, 90, 92]: Work in Garter stitch, increasing as follows:
Rows 9, 17, 25, 33, 41, 49, 57, 65, 73 and 81: Knit 1, increase 1, knit until there is 1 stitch left, increase 1, knit the last stitch. At the end of row 86 [88, 90, 92] you will have a total of 44 [46, 48, 50] stitches.
Bind off all stitches.

FINISHING

1.
Thread the tapestry needle with the same yarn that you used for your project and sew one of the shoulders: Place the front and back sides together, lining up the shoulder seams. Sew 21 [23, 23, 25] stitches from one of the shoulders.

2.
Pick up 54 [54, 58, 58] stitches around the neck (27 [27, 29, 29] from the front and 27 [27, 29, 29] from the back). Work 4 rows in 1x1 Rib stitch. Bind off.

Sew the ends of the neck seam and the second shoulder seam.

Sew the sleeves to the body of sweater, lining up the center of the sleeves with the shoulder seams.

we are knitters

3.
Next, sew the side seams and
sleeve seams.

4.
Weave in all ends.

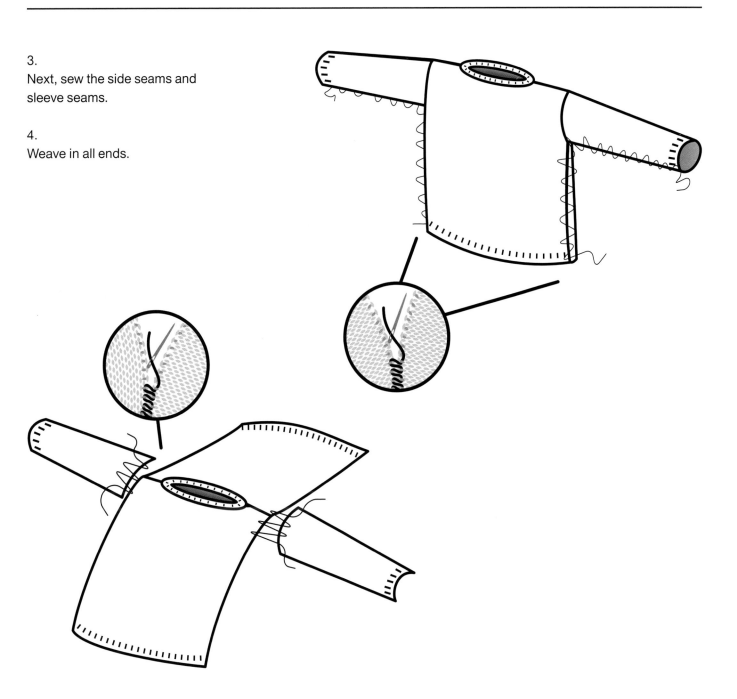

Bryant Scarf

LEVEL
Beginner

FINISHED MEASUREMENTS
8" (20 cm) wide x 90" (228 cm) long

YARN
We Are Knitters The Wool [100% Peruvian wool; 87 yards (80 meters)/200 grams]: 3 balls Turquoise

NEEDLES
One pair straight needles size US 19 (15 mm) Change needle size if necessary to obtain correct gauge.

NOTIONS
Tapestry needle

GAUGE
6 sts and 10 rows = 4" (10 cm) in Garter stitch (see page 35)

● *Stitches*
○ *Rows*

we are knitters

SCHEMATICS

20 cm | 8 in
12 ●

228 cm | 90 in
228 ○

START KNITTING

Cast on 12 stitches.
Work rows 1–228 in Garter stitch.
Bind off all stitches.

FINISHING

Weave in all ends.

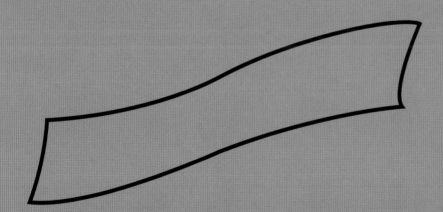

No. 2 Blanket

LEVEL
Easy

**FINISHED
MEASUREMENTS**
26" (67 cm) wide x 48"
(122 cm) long

YARN
We Are Knitters The
Wool [100% Peruvian
wool; 87 yards (80
meters)/200 grams]:
4 balls Salmon

NEEDLES
One 24" (60 cm) circular

needle size US 19
(15 mm)
Change needle size
if necessary to obtain
correct gauge.

NOTIONS
Tapestry needle

GAUGE
6 sts and 8 rows =
4" (10 cm) in Stockinette
stitch (see page 36)

● *Stitches*
○ *Rows*

SCHEMATICS

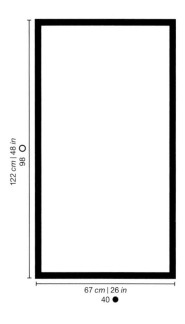

122 cm | 48 in
98 ○

67 cm | 26 in
40 ●

STITCH PATTERN
STOCKINETTE STITCH WITH CHECKS

Row 1: Knit.
Row 2 and all even rows: Knit 4, knit the stitches as they appear to last 4 stitches, knit 4.
Row 3: Knit 6, *purl 8, knit 2*; repeat from * to * 2 more times, end knit 4.
Rows 5, 7, and 9: Knit 6, *purl 2, knit 4, purl 2, and knit 2*; repeat from * to * 2 more times, end knit 4.

Row 11: Repeat row 3
Repeat rows 1–12 for Stockinette Stitch with Checks.

START KNITTING

Cast on 40 stitches.
Work rows 1–6 in Garter stitch (see page 35).
Rows 7–90: Work in Stockinette Stitch with Checks.
Row 91: Knit.
Row 92: Knit 4, purl 32, knit 4.
Rows 93–98: Work in Garter stitch.
Bind off all stitches.

FINISHING

Weave in all ends.

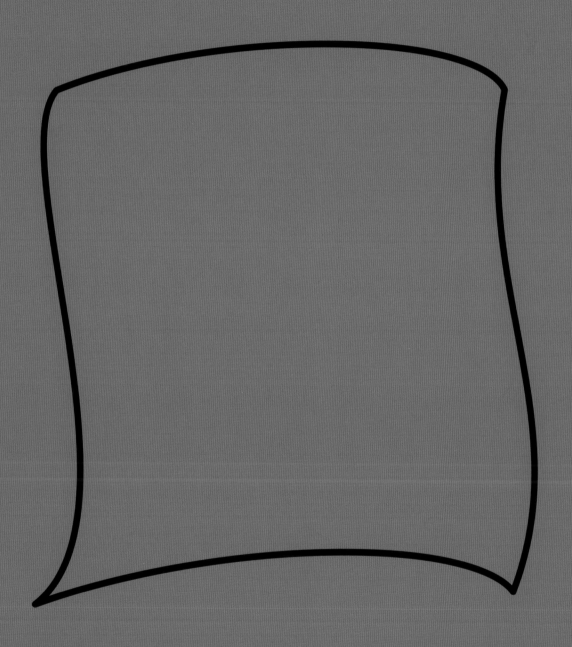

New York City

WHERE TO KNIT
The High Line: The former New York Central Railroad is now an elevated linear park on the west side of the city. Its benches, with beautiful views of the Hudson River, are perfect for knitting.

Madison Square Park: A personal favorite, located where Fifth Avenue and Broadway cross paths. You can knit here surrounded by squirrels and amazing views of the Empire State Building.

The Standard Hotel bar: Did we say fancy? You won't regret visiting their rooftop bar with views of the whole city. We can't deny having had one—or two—cocktails there while finishing our latest knitting project.

AVERAGE HIGH TEMPERATURES
Spring: 59.4°F (15.2°C)
Summer: 81.1°F (27.3°C)
Fall: 63.7°F (17.6°C)
Winter: 40.1°F (4.5°C)

RAINY SEASON
April

FAVORITE DISHES
Cheeseburger with fries
Everything bagel with cream cheese
Pastrami on rye

VEGGIE OPTIONS
Pizza slice
Falafel wrap

we are knitters

New York City: the city that started it all for us. A few years ago, we went to visit a friend of ours who was living in the Big Apple and noticed there was something going on: Yarn stores were everywhere, with amazing chunky wool in flashy colors (OMG), people were knitting in groups in cafés, and we even noticed a woman knitting on the subway.

Visiting NYC was definitely a WOW moment for us, since nothing like what we saw was happening back home. That trip was more than ten years ago, when knitting was not as popular as it is now, but there we were, watching people knitting in the most unexpected places in one of the biggest and most cosmopolitan cities in the world.

New York has always been a big source of #knitspiration for us. We even named a whole collection of kits after some of its most iconic landmarks. We kind of feel like we have a love story with the city (is that a thing? Whatever, it is for us), and every time we visit it feels like a second home. So, to all the New Yorkers reading these lines, you make New York a great place.

Now, please make room in your knitting wish list for these three patterns we shot in the City that Never Sleeps. To be honest, we could live all winter long in them: a cozy cardi, an extra-large scarf, and a big chunky beanie.

we are knitters

Martina Cardigan

LEVEL
Intermediate

SIZES
Small [Medium, Large, X-Large]

FINISHED MEASUREMENTS
41½ [42½, 44, 45½]" (106 [108, 112, 116] cm) bust

YARN
We Are Knitters The Petite Wool [100% Peruvian wool; 153 yards (140 meters)/100 grams]: 6 [6, 7, 7] balls Pearl

NEEDLES
One pair straight needles size US 11 (8 mm) Change needle size if necessary to obtain correct gauge.

NOTIONS
Stitch holders; tapestry needle

GAUGE
12 sts and 24 rows = 4" (10 cm) in Garter stitch (see page 35)

● *Stitches*
○ *Rows*

SCHEMATICS

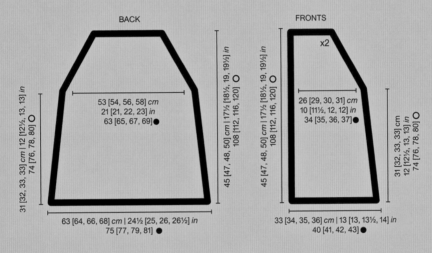

BACK

53 [54, 56, 58] cm
21 [21, 22, 23] in
63 [65, 67, 69] ●

31 [32, 33, 33] cm | 12 [12½, 13, 13] in
74 [76, 78, 80] ○

45 [47, 48, 50] cm | 17½ [18½, 19, 19½] in
108 [112, 116, 120] ○

63 [64, 66, 68] cm | 24½ [25, 26, 26½] in
75 [77, 79, 81] ●

FRONTS

x2

26 [29, 30, 31] cm
10 [11½, 12, 12] in
34 [35, 36, 37] ●

45 [47, 48, 50] cm | 17½ [18½, 19, 19½] in
108 [112, 116, 120] ○

31 [32, 33, 33] cm
12 [12½, 13, 13] in
74 [76, 78, 80] ○

33 [34, 35, 36] cm | 13 [13, 13½, 14] in
40 [41, 42, 43] ●

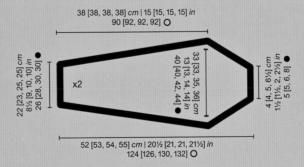

SLEEVES

38 [38, 38, 38] cm | 15 [15, 15, 15] in
90 [92, 92, 92] ○

x2

22 [23, 25, 25] cm
8½ [9, 10, 10] in
26 [28, 30, 30] ●

33 [33, 35, 36] cm
13 [13, 14, 14] in
40 [40, 42, 44] ●

4 [4, 5, 6½] cm
1½ [1½, 2, 2½] in
5 [5, 6, 8] ●

52 [53, 54, 55] cm | 20½ [21, 21, 21½] in
124 [126, 130, 132] ○

START KNITTING

BACK
Cast on 75 [77, 79, 81] stitches.
Work rows 1–74 [76, 78, 80] in Garter stitch, decreasing as follows:
Row 1 and unspecified rows: knit all stitches.
Rows 13, 23, 33, 43, 53, and 63: Knit 2, knit 2 together, knit until there are 4 stitches left, knit 2 together, knit the last 2 stitches. At the end of row 63 you will have a total of 63 [65, 67, 69] stitches.
Work rows 75 [77, 79, 81]–108 [112, 116, 120] in Garter stitch, shaping the raglan as follows.

SIZE S

Rows 75, 77, 79, 81, and 83: Repeat row 13. At the end of row 83 you will have a total of 53 stitches.
Row 76 and all even rows: Knit all stitches.
Row 85: Knit 2, knit 2 together, knit 2 together, knit until there are 6 stitches left, knit 2 together, knit 2 together, knit the last 2 stitches. You will have a total of 49 stitches.
Rows 87, 89, 91, 93, 95, 97, 99, 101, 103, 105, and 107: Repeat row 13. At the end of row 107 you will have a total of 27 stitches.
Leave the stitches on hold.

SIZE M

Row 77 and all odd rows: Repeat row 13. At the end of row 111 you will have a total of 29 stitches.
Row 78 and all even rows: Knit all stitches.
Leave the stitches on hold.

SIZE L

Rows 79, 81, 83, 85, 87, 89, 91, 93, and 95: Repeat row 13. At the end of row 95 you will have a total of 49 stitches.
Row 80 and all even rows: Knit all stitches.
Row 97: Knit all stitches.
Rows 99, 101, 103, 105, 107, 109, 111, 113, and 115: Repeat row 13. At the end of row 115 you will have a total of 31 stitches.
Leave the stitches on hold.

SIZE XL

Rows 81, 83, 85, 87, 89, and 91: Repeat row 13.
Row 82 and all even rows: knit all stitches.
Rows 95, 97, 99, 101, and 103: Repeat row 13.
Row 105: Knit all stitches.
Rows 107, 109, 111, 113, 115, 117, and 119: Repeat row 13. At the end of row 119 you will have a total of 33 stitches.
Leave the stitches on hold.

LEFT FRONT

Cast on 40 [41, 42, 43] stitches.

Work rows 1–74 [76, 78, 80] in Garter stitch, decreasing as follows: Rows 13, 23, 33, 43, 53, and 63: Knit 2, knit 2 together, knit the remaining stitches. At the end of row 63 you will have a total of 34 [35, 36, 37] stitches.

Work rows 75 [77, 79, 81]–108 [112, 116, 120] in Garter stitch, shaping the raglan as follows:

RIGHT FRONT

Cast on 40 [41, 42, 43] stitches.

Rows 1 to 108 [112, 116, 121] work as for the Left Front.

Row 109 [113, 117, 121]: Knit.

Leave the stitches on hold.

SIZE S

Rows 75, 77, 79, 81, and 83: Repeat row 13. At the end of row 83 you will have a total of 29 stitches

Row 76 and all even rows: Knit all stitches.

Row 85: Knit 2, knit 2 together, knit 2 together, knit the remaining stitches. You will have a total of 27 stitches.

Rows 87, 89, 91, 93, 95, 97, 99, 101, 103, 105, and 107: Repeat row 13. At the end of row 107 you will have a total of 16 stitches.

Leave the stitches on hold.

SIZE M

Row 77 and all odd rows: Repeat row 13. At the end of row 111 you will have a total of 17 stitches.

Row 78 and all even rows: Knit all stitches.

Leave the stitches on hold.

SIZE L

Rows 79, 81, 83, 85, 87, 89, 91, 93, and 95: Repeat row 13. At the end of row 95 you will have a total of 27 stitches.

Row 80 and all even rows: Knit all stitches.

Row 97: Knit all stitches.

Rows 99, 101, 103, 105, 107, 109, 111, 113, and 115: Repeat row 13. At the end of row 115 you will have a total of 18 stitches.

Leave the stitches on hold.

SIZE XL

Rows 81, 83, 85, 87, 89, 91, 95, 97, 99, 101, and 103: Repeat row 13. At the end of row 103 you will have a total of 26 stitches.

Row 82 and all even rows: Knit all stitches.

Row 105: Knit all stitches.

Rows 107, 109, 111, 113, 115, 117, and 119: Repeat row 13. At the end of row 119 you will have a total of 19 stitches.

Leave the stitches on hold.

SLEEVES

Follow these instructions twice to make two sleeves.
Cast on 26 [28, 30, 30] stitches.
Work rows 1–90 [92, 92, 92] in Garter stitch,
increasing as follows:

SIZE S

Rows 13, 25, 37, 49, 61, 73, and 85: Knit 1, increase 1, knit until there is 1 stitch left, increase 1, knit the last stitch. At the end of row 90 you will have a total of 40 stitches.

SIZE M

Rows 13, 29, 43, 59, 75, and 91: Knit 1, increase 1, knit until there is 1 stitch left, increase 1, knit the last stitch. At the end of row 92 you will have a total of 40 stitches.

SIZE L

Rows 13, 29, 43, 59, 75, and 91: Knit 1, increase 1, knit until there is 1 stitch left, increase 1, knit the last stitch. At the end of row 92 you will have a total of 42 stitches.

SIZE XL

Rows 13, 21, 29, 43, 59, 75, and 91: Knit 1, increase 1, knit until there is 1 stitch left, increase 1, knit the last stitch. At the end of row 92 you will have a total of 44 stitches.

ALL SIZES

Work rows 91 [93, 93, 93]–124 [128, 130, 132] in Garter stitch, shaping the raglan as follows:

SIZE S

Rows 91, 93, 95, 97, and 99: Knit 2, knit 2 together, knit until there are 4 stitches left, knit 2 together, knit the last 2 stitches. At the end of row 99 you will have a total of 30 stitches.
Row 92 and all even rows: Knit all stitches.
Row 101: Knit 2, knit 2 together, knit 2 together, knit until there are 6 stitches left, knit 2 together, knit 2 together, knit the last 2 stitches. You will have a total of 26 stitches.
Rows 103, 105, 107, 109, 111, 113, 115, 117, 119, and 121: Knit 2, knit 2 together, knit until there are 4 stitches left, knit 2 together, knit the last 2 stitches. At the end of row 121 you will have a total of 6 stitches.
Row 123: Knit 2, knit 2 together, knit 2. You will have a total of 5 stitches. Leave the stitches on hold.

SIZE M

Rows 93 and all odd rows through row 125: Knit 2, knit 2 together, knit until there are 4 stitches left, knit 2 together, knit the last 2 stitches. At the end of row 125 you will have a total of 6 stitches.
Row 94 and all even rows: Knit all stitches.
Row 127: Knit 2, knit 2 together, knit 2. You will have a total of 5 stitches. Leave the stitches on hold.

SIZE L

Rows 93, 95, 97, 99, 101, 103, 105, 107, and 109: Knit 2, knit 2 together, knit until there are 4 stitches left, knit 2 together, knit the last 2 stitches. At the end of row 109 you will have a total of 24 stitches.
Row 94 and all even rows: Knit all stitches.
Row 111: Knit all stitches.
Rows 113, 115, 117, 119, 121, 123, 125, 127, and 129: Knit 2, knit 2 together, knit until there are 4 stitches

left, knit 2 together, knit the last 2 stitches. At the end of row 129 you will have a total of 6 stitches. Leave the stitches on hold.

SIZE XL
Rows 93, 95, 97, 99, 101, and 103: Knit 2, knit 2 together, knit until there are 4 stitches left, knit 2 together, knit the last 2 stitches. At the end of row 103 you will have a total of 32 stitches.
Row 94 and all even rows: Knit all stitches.
Row 105: Knit all stitches.
Rows 107, 109, 111, 113, and 115: Knit 2, knit 2 together, knit until there are 4 stitches left, knit 2 together, knit the last 2 stitches. At the end of row 115 you will have a total of 22 stitches.
Row 117: Knit all stitches.
Rows 119, 121, 123, 125, 127, 129, and 131: Knit 2, knit 2 together, knit until there are 4 stitches left, knit 2 together, knit the last 2 stitches. At the end of row 131 you will have a total of 8 stitches.
Leave the stitches on hold.

NECK
Place all of the pieces on the needle in the following order with right sides facing out. Left Front, one sleeve, Back, another sleeve, and Right Front.

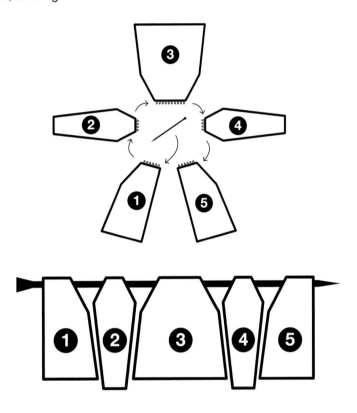

Row 1: Knit 15 [16, 17, 18], knit 2 together, knit 3 [3, 4, 6], knit 2 together, knit 25 [27, 29, 31], knit 2 together, knit 3 [3, 4, 6], knit 2 together, knit 15 [16, 17, 18]. You will have a total of 65 [69, 75, 83] stitches.

Rows 2 and 4: Knit.
Row 3: Knit 14 [15, 16, 17], knit 2 together, knit 3 [3, 4, 6], knit 2 together, knit 23 [25, 27, 29], knit 2 together, knit 3 [3, 4, 6], knit 2 together, knit 14 [15, 16, 17]. You will have a total of 61 [65, 71, 79] stitches.

Row 5: Knit 13 [14, 15, 16], knit 2 together, knit 3 [3, 4, 6], knit 2 together, knit 21 [23, 25, 27], knit 2 together, knit 3 [3, 4, 6], knit 2 together, knit 13 [14, 15, 16]. You will have a total of 57 [61, 67, 75] stitches.
Bind off all stitches.

FINISHING

Join the sleeves to the Front and Back: Thread the tapestry needle with the same yarn used in the sweater and insert it into the middle of the first stitch of the sleeve and pull it out through the second stitch. Then insert the needle into the first stitch from the front and pull it out through the second stitch. Continue like this, alternating between the sleeve and the front.

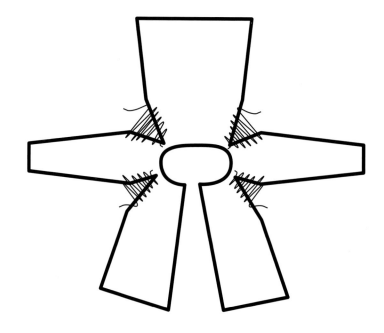

Sew the side seams and the sleeves using Mattress stitch (see page 56).
Weave in all ends.

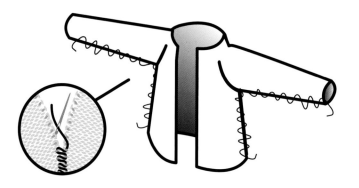

we are knitters

Viti Scarf

LEVEL
Intermediate

FINISHED MEASUREMENTS
9" (23 cm) wide x
86" (218 cm) long,
excluding fringe

YARN
We Are Knitters The
Petite Wool [100%
Peruvian wool; 153 yards
(140 meters)/100 grams]:
4 balls Spotted Blue

NEEDLES
One pair straight needles
size US 11 (8 mm)

Change needle size
if necessary to obtain
correct gauge.

NOTIONS
Cable needle; tapestry
needle

GAUGE
12 sts and 18 rows =
4" (10 cm) in Garter stitch
(see page 35)

● *Stitches*
○ *Rows*

we are knitters

SCHEMATICS

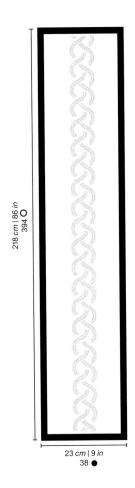

218 cm | 86 in
394 ○

23 cm | 9 in
38 ●

START KNITTING

Cast on 38 stitches.
Rows 1, 2, 3, and 4: Knit 10, *knit 3, purl 3*; repeat from * to * until there are 10 stitches left, knit to end.
Row 5: Knit 10, slip the next 6 stitches to a cable needle and leave them on hold in *front* of your work, knit 3, purl 3, slip the held stitches back to the left-hand needle, knit 3, purl 3, knit 3, purl 3, knit to end.
Rows 6, 7, and 8: Repeat row 1.
Row 9: Knit 13, purl 3, slip the next 6 stitches to a cable needle and leave them on hold at the *back* of your work, knit 3, purl 3, slip the held stitches back to the left-hand needle, knit 3, purl 3, knit to end.
Repeat rows 2–9 until you've worked 394 rows.
Bind off all stitches.

FINISHING

Weave in all ends.

Fringe:
Cut lengths of yarn about 12" (30.5 cm) and tie them onto the edges of the scarf.

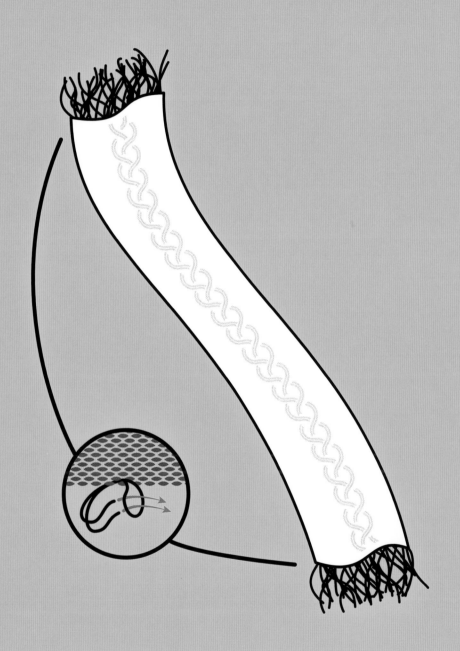

Akan Beanie

LEVEL
Intermediate

SIZES
One size

FINISHED MEASUREMENTS
27" (69 cm) brim circumference

YARN
We Are Knitters The Wool [100% Peruvian wool; 87 yards (80 meters)/200 grams]: 1 ball Denim

NEEDLES
One pair straight needles size US 19 (15 mm)

Change needle size if necessary to obtain correct gauge.

NOTIONS
Cable needle; tapestry needle; 2 cardboard circles about 4" (10 cm) in diameter, with a 2" (5 cm) hole cut out of their centers; scissors

GAUGE
6 sts and 8 rows = 4" (10 cm) in Stockinette stitch (see page 36)

● *Stitches*
○ *Rows*

SCHEMATICS

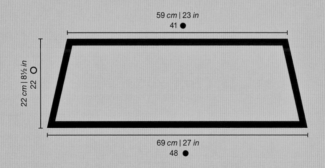

59 cm | 23 in
41 ●

22 cm | 8½ in
22 ○

69 cm | 27 in
48 ●

START KNITTING

Cast on 48 stitches.

Row 1 and all odd rows: Purl 1, *slip 2 stitches to a cable needle and leave them on hold in *front* of your work, knit 2, slip the held stitches back to the left-hand needle, knit 2, purl 2*; repeat from * to * until 5 stitches remain, slip 2 stitches to a cable needle and leave them on hold in *front* of your work, knit 2, slip the held stitches back to the left-hand needle, knit 2, purl 1.

Row 2 and all even rows: Knit 1, purl 4, *knit 2, purl 4*; repeat from * to * until 1 stitch remains, and knit it. Repeat rows 1 and 2 until you have worked 18 rows.

Row 19: Purl 1, *slip 2 stitches to a cable needle and leave them on hold in *front* of your work, knit 2, slip the held stitches back to the left-hand needle, knit 2, purl 2 together*; repeat from * to * until 5 stitches remain, slip 2 stitches to a cable needle and leave them on hold in *front* of your work, knit 2, slip the held stitches back to the left-hand needle, knit 2, purl 1. You will have a total of 41 stitches.

Rows 20 and 22: *Knit 1, purl 4*; repeat from * to * until 1 stitch remains, and purl it.

Row 21: *Purl 1, slip 2 stitches to a cable needle and leave them on hold in *front* of your work, knit 2, slip the held stitches back to the left-hand needle, knit 2*; repeat from * to * until 1 stitch remains, and purl it.

FINISHING

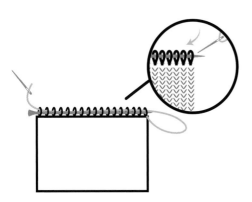

Cut the yarn, leaving enough length to sew the side of the beanie plus some extra. Thread the yarn onto the tapestry needle and draw the needle through each of the stitches

on the needle, removing them from the needle. Pull tightly to cinch the top of the beanie.

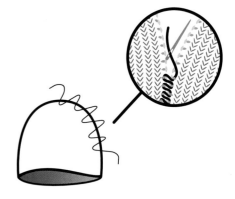

Sew the side seam using Mattress stitch (see page 56).
Weave in all ends.

we are knitters

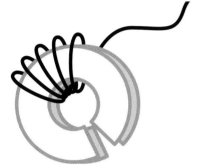

1.
Cut a small wedge out of both cardboard circles. Hold the two cardboard circles together and completely wrap them with wool.

2.
Cut between the two circles, cutting the wrapped yarn.

3.
Slightly separate the two circles and tie the center of the pom-pom with a length of yarn about 24" (61 cm) long to secure. Remove the cardboard circles.

4.
Trim the pom-pom as needed to get a rounded shape, leaving the yarn that was used to secure the pom-pom untrimmed to sew the pom-pom to the top of the hat.

Madrid

WHERE TO KNIT
Parque de El Retiro: The biggest park in the city. The perfect place to take a walk or go for a boat ride on the lake. You can always lie under the shade of the trees and have a little siesta, too!

Círculo de Bellas Artes: Founded in 1880, it is an arts center where poets, writers, and artists used to meet more than a century ago. They have a big terrace, perfect to chill on while having a coffee and, why not, knitting.

Malasaña: A very hip area, it's full of trendy shops, restaurants, and bars. We recommend you visit during the day but come back at night, too. It's always so full of life.

AVERAGE HIGH TEMPERATURES
Spring: 65.3°F (18.5°C)
Summer: 87.1°F (30.6°C)
Fall: 68.5°F (20.3°C)
Winter: 51.8°F (11.0°C)

RAINY SEASON
March and April

FAVORITE DISHES
Paella
Huevos rotos
Croquetas

VEGGIE OPTIONS
Gazpacho
Tortilla de patata

we are knitters

Madrid! Our beloved hometown and the home of the WAK headquarters! Since we first started, the craft scene in Madrid has changed a lot. It didn't used to be very exciting, but as the years have passed, it has become a city with lots of yarn stores and small businesses owned by makers, and it is no longer rare to see knitting parties in the trendy areas of Malasaña or Salesas. Spain has always been a country where craftsmanship has had a big presence (*mantillas* in Andalucía, espadrilles in the Balearic Islands, and *encaje de bolillos* in Castilla, all of them handmade by local artisans), and we love being a part of the movement that shares these skills with a new generation.

If you ask us, what makes Madrid a great place (apart from the ever-blue sky) is its people. They say you can go to Madrid all by yourself and you will leave with a bunch of *amigos* for life. Trust us, that's a fact! We've seen so many strangers become best friends at our knitting events. Maybe the sangria has something to do with it—but either way, the people of Madrid will welcome anyone with open arms.

In this section, you'll find three friendly patterns: a scarf, a headband, and a pillow.

patterns — madrid

Encina Scarf

LEVEL
Easy

FINISHED MEASUREMENTS
84" (213 cm) wingspan x 31½" (80 cm) at center spine

YARN
We Are Knitters The Meriwool [100% merino wool; 148 yards (136 meters)/100 grams]: 6 balls Mustard

NEEDLES
One pair of straight needles size US 8 (5 mm) Change needle size if necessary to obtain correct gauge.

NOTIONS
Stitch marker; tapestry needle

GAUGE
16 sts and 18 rows = 4" (10 cm) in Stockinette stitch (see page 36)

● *Stitches*
○ *Rows*

patterns — madrid

SPECIAL TECHNIQUES

Yarnover:
See page 47.

Work 1 stitch 3 times:
This is a double increase. Insert the needle and draw up a loop as if to knit but do not drop the stitch from the left-hand needle. Bring the working yarn to the front and purl that same stitch, then bring the yarn to the back and knit it again. Drop the original stitch from the left-hand needle; you will have 3 stitches on the right-hand needle.

START KNITTING

Cast on 1 stitch.
Row 1: Work 1 stitch 3 times. You will have a total of 3 stitches.
Row 2: Knit 1, work 1 stitch 3 times, knit 1. You will have a total of 5 stitches.
Row 3: Knit 2, yarn over, knit 1, yarn over, knit 2. You will have a total of 7 stitches.
Rows 4, 6, 8, 10, and 12: Knit.
Row 5: Knit 3, yarn over, knit 1, yarn over, knit 3. You will have a total of 9 stitches.
Row 7: Knit 3, yarn over, knit 1, yarn over, place a stitch marker, knit 1, yarn over, knit 1, yarn over, knit 3. You will have a total of 13 stitches.
Row 9 and all remaining odd rows:

Knit 3, yarn over, knit to stitch marker, yarn over, slip the stitch marker, knit 1, yarn over, knit until 3 stitches remain, yarn over, knit 3.
Rows 14 and 16: Knit 3, purl until 1 stitch before the stitch marker, knit 1, slip the stitch marker, purl until 3 stitches remain, knit 3.
Rows 18, 20, and 22: Knit.
Rows 24 and 26: Knit 3, purl until 1 stitch before the stitch marker, knit 1, slip the stitch marker, purl until 3 stitches remain, knit 3.
Repeat rows 17 to 26 until you've worked 172 rows total. You will have a total of 341 stitches.
Bind off all stitches.

FINISHING

Weave in all ends.

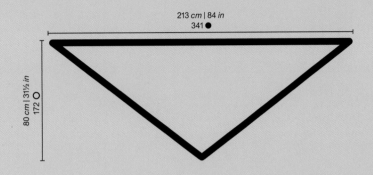

213 *cm* | 84 *in*
341 ●

80 *cm* | 31½ *in*
172 ○

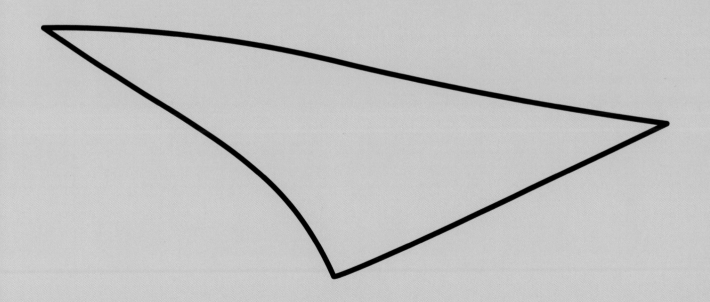

Olmo Headband

LEVEL
Easy

SIZES
One size

FINISHED MEASUREMENTS
1½" (4 cm) wide x 19½" (49 cm) long

YARN
We Are Knitters The Petite Wool [100% Peruvian wool; 153 yards (140 meters)/100 grams]: 1 ball Beige

NEEDLES
One pair straight needles size US 11 (8 mm)

Change needle size if necessary to obtain correct gauge.

NOTIONS
Stitch holders; tapestry needle

GAUGE
12 sts and 16 rows = 4" (10 cm) in Stockinette stitch (see page 36)

NOTE
This headband is constructed of 3 strands of I-cord, each worked separately from one long cast-on, which are then braided and seamed.

● *Stitches*
○ *Rows*

SCHEMATICS

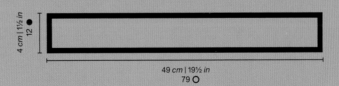

4 cm | 1½ in
12 ●

49 cm | 19½ in
79 ○

START KNITTING

Cast on 12 stitches.

Row 1: Knit 4.

Continue working only these 4 stitches in I-cord, leaving the remaining stitches on hold.

Rows 2–78: Do not turn your work. Slip the 4 stitches you just worked from the right-hand needle to the left-hand needle. Knit 4.

Leave these 4 stitches on hold.

Pick up the next 4 stitches that you had on hold at the beginning of your work, leaving the last 4 stitches on hold. Repeat rows 2–78 with these 4 stitches.

Leave these 4 stitches on hold.

Pick up the last 4 stitches that you had on hold at the beginning of your work. Repeat rows 2–78 with these 4 stitches.

Braid the three strands together.

Row 79: Place all 12 stitches on one needle, knit 1 row.

Bind off all stitches.

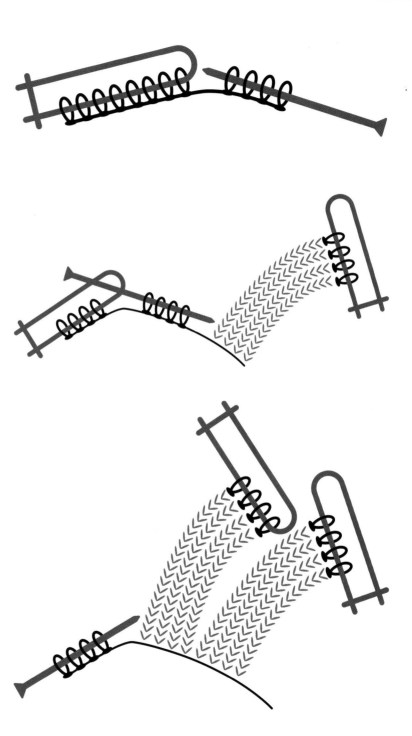

we are knitters

FINISHING

Sew the ends together: Thread the tapestry needle with the same yarn used for your project and sew with a zigzag stitch, picking up one stitch from each end of the headband, as shown.

Weave in all ends.

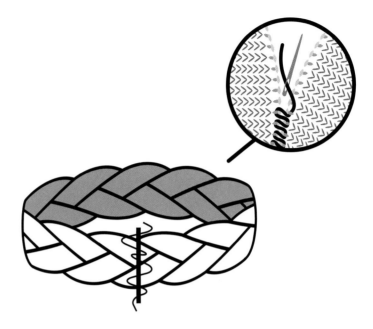

Pino Pillow

LEVEL
Beginner

FINISHED MEASUREMENTS
17½" (45 cm) square

YARN
We Are Knitters The Wool [100% Peruvian wool; 87 yards (80 meters)/200 grams]: 3 balls Spotted Grey

NEEDLES
One pair straight needles size US 19 (15 mm)

Change needle size if necessary to obtain correct gauge.

NOTIONS
Tapestry needle; 18" (46 cm) pillow form or stuffing; crochet hook size US P/Q (15 mm) or slightly smaller, for fringe (optional)

GAUGE
6 sts and 9 rows = 4" (10 cm) in Stockinette stitch (see page 36)

● *Stitches*
○ *Rows*

SCHEMATICS

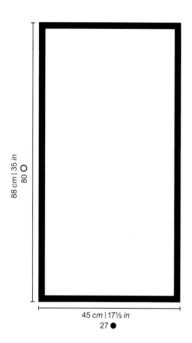

88 cm | 35 in
80 O

45 cm | 17½ in
27 ●

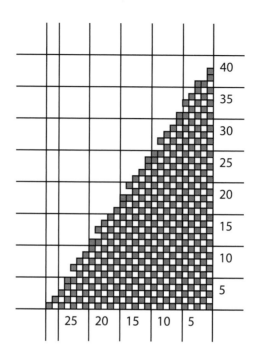

40
35
30
25
20
15
10
5

25 20 15 10 5

NOTE: Gray boxes indicate knot placement for fringe.

START KNITTING

Cast on 27 stitches.
Rows 1–80:
Work in Stockinette stitch.
Bind off all stitches.

FINISHING

Fold the piece in half with the right side out as shown. Thread the tapestry needle with the same yarn used for the project and sew the side seams with a zigzag stitch as shown.

Fill your cushion with a pillow form, stuffing, or even scraps of yarn until you have the desired shape and fullness.

Sew the top of your cushion closed.

Make a knot and draw the ends into the cushion to hide.

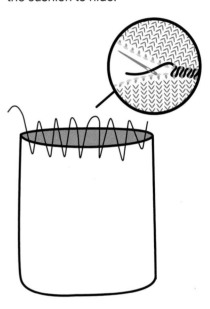

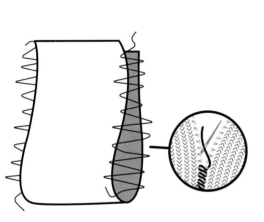

FRINGE

Cut strands about 7" (18 cm) long and tie them at the places indicated in the diagram. You can insert a crochet hook under the stitch to catch the loop, then insert the loose ends through the loop.

Cartagena de Indias

WHERE TO KNIT
La Cevichería: Good restaurant with an outdoor terrace. A great place to have an appetizer and a drink when the heat starts to hit.

Café del Mar: An outdoor bar with amazing views of the ocean. A perfect mix of Latin music and an electro-chill DJ set. Best time to visit: sunset.

Getsemaní: Possibly the hippest area in the city. It will probably be full of local people whenever you visit. Its little houses in different colors, restaurants, and bars make it one of the most enjoyable places to visit in the city.

AVERAGE HIGH TEMPERATURES
Spring: 88.3°F (31.3°C)
Summer: 89.2°F (31.8°C)
Fall: 88.3°F (31.3°C)
Winter: 87.8°F (31.0°C)

RAINY SEASON
September through October

FAVORITE DISHES
Arepas
Ajiaco
Bandeja paisa

VEGGIE OPTIONS
Arroz de coco

we are knitters

We'll be honest: WAK has no personal connection to Colombia. But that doesn't mean we don't appreciate all the beauty it has to offer! Makers can spot other makers when they see them, and that's what happens when you go to Colombia, especially to Cartagena de Indias.

First up, their artisan crafts! You can find everything from *mochilas*, sombreros *vueltiaos*, and ponchos to ceramics, filigree jewelry from Mompox, and *werregue* baskets. There is so much to explore here.

Then, there are the colors! Like many cities in South America, Cartagena is an explosion of color. Most buildings have one or two floors, each painted in a different shade. Add to those vivid hues the beauty of gigantic bougainvillea, and your life will never be the same. The city center, a trendy area called Getsemaní, is a clear example of color-on-color magic.

Finally, there's the lifestyle. The vibe in Colombia is so chill that it is impossible not to relax once you are there. Maybe it is because of the super hot and humid weather 365 days a year. Or maybe it is because of the mojitos you can have almost everywhere. We'll never know, because you can't seem to have one without the other.

Don't expect big chunky knits in this section—instead you'll find two super light and fresh tees to knit in cotton that will make your life easier (*waaaaaay* easier) when on vacation during the summer.

LA Tank

LEVEL
Intermediate

SIZES
Small [Medium, Large, X-Large]

FINISHED MEASUREMENTS
35 [38, 41, 44]" (88 [96, 104, 112] cm) bust

YARN
We Are Knitters The Pima Cotton [100% pima cotton; 232 yards (212 meters)/100 grams]: 2 [2, 3, 3] balls Natural

NEEDLES
One pair straight needles size US 8 (5 mm) Change needle size if necessary to obtain correct gauge.

NOTIONS
Stitch holders; tapestry needle

GAUGE
18 sts and 23 rows = 4" (10 cm) in reverse Stockinette stitch (see page 37)

● *Stitches*
○ *Rows*

139

SCHEMATICS

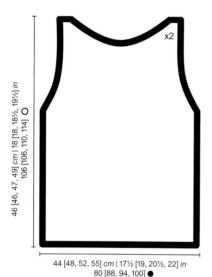

46 [46, 47, 49] cm | 18 [18, 18½, 19½] in
106 [106, 110, 114] ○

44 [48, 52, 55] cm | 17½ [19, 20½, 22] in
80 [88, 94, 100] ●

START KNITTING

FRONT

Cast on 80 [88, 94, 100] stitches. Work rows 1–12 in 1x1 Rib stitch (see page 38).

Rows 13–68: Work in reverse Stockinette stitch (purl odd rows, knit even rows).

Rows 69–80: Continue working in reverse Stockinette stitch, shaping for armholes as follows:

Row 69: Bind off 3 stitches, purl to end. You will have a total of 77 [85, 91, 97] stitches.

Row 70: Bind off 3 stitches, knit to end. You will have a total of 74 [82, 88, 94] stitches.

Rows 71, 73, 75, and 77: Bind off 2 stitches, purl to end. At the end of row 77 you will have a total of 60 [68, 74, 80] stitches.

Rows 72, 74, 76, and 78: Bind off 2 stitches, knit to end. At the end of row 78 you will have a total of 58 [66, 72, 78] stitches.

Row 79: Bind off 1 stitch, purl to end. You will have a total of 57 [65, 71, 77] stitches.

Row 80: Bind off 1 stitch, knit the rest of the stitches. You will have a total of 56 [64, 70, 76] stitches.

Rows 81–86 [86, 88, 90]: Work in reverse Stockinette stitch.

Rows 87 [87, 89, 91]–106 [106, 110, 114]: Continue working in reverse Stockinette stitch, splitting for the neck and working as follows:

Row 87 [87, 89, 91]: Purl 22 [25, 26, 27], bind off 12 [14, 18, 22] stitches, purl to end.

Leave the first 22 [25, 26, 27] stitches on hold.

Row 89 [89, 91, 93]: Bind off 3 stitches, purl to end. You will have a total of 19 [22, 23, 24] stitches.

Rows 91 [91, 93, 95], 93 [93, 95, 97], 95 [95, 97, 99], and 97 [97, 99, 101]: Bind off 2 stitches, purl to end. At the end of row 97 [97, 99, 101] you will have a total of 11 [14, 15, 16] stitches.

Row 99 [99, 101, 103] and all odd rows: purl all stitches.

Bind off all 11 [14, 15, 16] stitches.

Transfer the 22 [25, 26, 27] held stitches to a needle and work rows 88 [88, 90, 92]–106 [106, 110, 114] in reverse Stockinette stitch as follows:

Row 88 [88, 90, 92]: Bind off 3 stitches, knit to end. You will have a total of 19 [22, 23, 24] stitches.

Row 89 [89, 91, 93] and all odd rows: Purl.

Rows 90 [90, 92, 94], 92 [92, 94, 96], 94 [94, 96, 98], and 96 [96, 98, 100]: Bind off 2 stitches, knit to end. At the end of row 96 [96, 98, 100] you will have a total of 11 [14, 15, 16] stitches.

Row 98 [98, 100, 102] and all even rows: Knit all stitches.

Bind off all stitches.

START KNITTING (CONTINUED)

BACK

Work through row 80 the same as for the Front.

Work rows 81–90 [90, 92, 94] in reverse Stockinette stitch.

Rows 91 [91, 93, 95]–106 [106, 110, 114]: Continue working in reverse Stockinette stitch, splitting for the neck and working as follows:

Row 91 [91, 93, 95]: Purl 22 [25, 26, 27], bind off 12 [14, 18, 22] stitches, purl to end.

Leave the first 22 [25, 26, 27] stitches on hold.

Row 93 [93, 95, 97]: Bind off 3 stitches, purl to end. You will have a total of 19 [22, 23, 24] stitches.

Rows 95 [95, 97, 99], 97 [97, 99, 101], 99 [99, 101, 103], and 101 [101, 103, 105]: Bind off 2 stitches, purl to end. At the end of row 101 [101, 103, 105] you will have a total of 11 [14, 15, 16] stitches.

Row 103 [103, 105, 107] and all odd rows: Purl all stitches.

Bind off all 11 [14, 15, 16] stitches. Transfer the 22 [25, 26, 27] held stitches to a needle and work rows 92 [92, 94, 96]–106 [106, 110, 114] in reverse Stockinette stitch as follows:

Row 92 [92, 94, 96]: Bind off 3 stitches, knit to end. You will have a total of 21 [22, 23, 24] stitches.

Rows 94 [94, 96, 98], 96 [96, 98, 100], 98 [98, 100, 102], and 100 [100, 102, 104]: Bind off 2 stitches, knit to end. At the end of row 100 [100, 102, 104] you will have a total of 11 [14, 15, 16] stitches.

Row 102 [102, 104, 106] and all even rows: Knit all stitches.

Bind off all stitches.

FINISHING

1.

Thread the tapestry needle with the same yarn used for the project and sew one of the shoulders: Place the front and back with the wrong sides together, lining up the shoulder seams. Sew 11 [14, 15, 16] stitches from one of the shoulders.

2.

Pick up and knit 124 [124, 140, 156] stitches around the neck (66 [66, 74, 82] from the front and 58 [58, 66, 74] from the back). Knit 1 row. Bind off all picked-up stitches.

3.

Sew the ends of the neck seam and the second shoulder seam.

4.

Starting at the first armhole decrease and working up and over the shoulder to the other side, pick up 3 stitches in the bound-off stitches and 1 stitch in 1 row, *pick up 2 stitches in the bound-off stitches, pick up 1 stitch in 1 row*; repeat from * to * 3 more times. Pick up 1 stitch in 1 row. **Skip 1 row, pick up 4 stitches in next 4 rows**; repeat from ** to ** 9 [9, 11, 13] more times. Skip 1 row, pick up 3 [3, 2, 0] stitches in next 3 [3, 2, 0] rows, pick up 1 stitch in the next bound-off stitch, pick up 1 stitch in 1 row. Repeat from * to * 4 more times, pick up 3 stitches in the last bind-off stitches. You will have a total of 77 [77, 84, 90] stitches. Knit 1 row.
Bind off all stitches.
Repeat for the other armhole.
Sew the side seams and sleeve seams with a zigzag stitch.

5.

Weave in all ends.

Lindy Top

LEVEL
Intermediate

SIZES
Small [Medium, Large, X-Large]

FINISHED MEASUREMENTS
33 [36, 39, 43]" (84 [90, 100, 108] cm) bust

YARN
We Are Knitters The Pima Cotton [100% pima cotton; 232 yards (212 meters)/100 grams]: 3 balls Light Salmon

NEEDLES
One 31½" (80 cm) circular needle size US 8 (5 mm)

Change needle size if necessary to obtain correct gauge.

NOTIONS
Stitch holders; tapestry needle

GAUGE
18 sts and 23 rows = 4" (10 cm) in Stockinette stitch (see page 36)

NOTE
Circular needle is used to accommodate the number of stitches on the needle; do not join.

● *Stitches*
○ *Rows*

SCHEMATICS

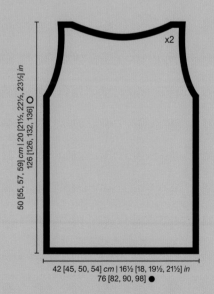

50 [55, 57 , 59] *cm* | 20 [21½, 22½, 23½] *in*
126 [126, 132, 136] ○

x2

42 [45, 50, 54] *cm* | 16½ [18, 19½, 21½] *in*
76 [82, 90, 98] ●

□	Odd rows=Knit 1. Even rows=Purl 1.
⊟	Odd rows=Purl 1. Even rows=Knit 1.
O	Yarn over
╲	Slip, knit, pass over
╱	Knit 2 together

we are knitters

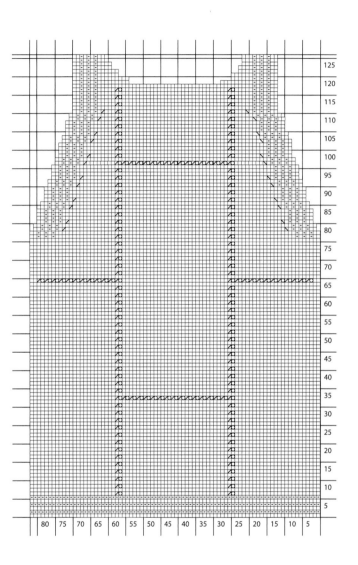

□ *Odd rows=Knit 1.*
  Even rows=Purl 1.

⊡ *Odd rows=Purl 1.*
  Even rows=Knit 1.

○ *Yarn over*

╲ *Slip, knit, pass over*

╱ *Knit 2 together*

patterns — cartagena de indias

147

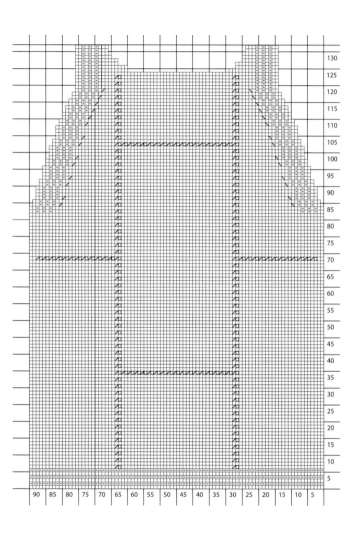

□ *Odd rows=Knit 1.*
  Even rows=Purl 1.

⊟ *Odd rows=Purl 1.*
  Even rows=Knit 1.

○ *Yarn over*

╲ *Slip, knit, pass over*

╱ *Knit 2 together*

we are knitters

XL

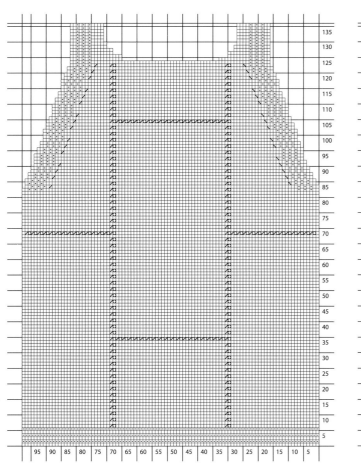

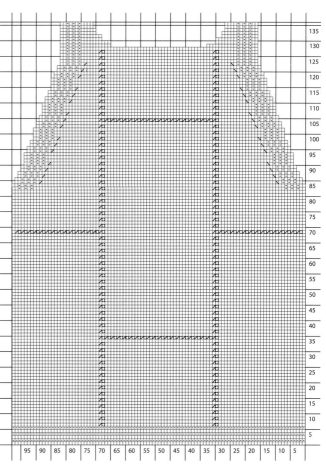

☐ *Odd rows=Knit 1.*
Even rows=Purl 1.

⊟ *Odd rows=Purl 1.*
Even rows=Knit 1.

○ *Yarn over*

╲ *Slip, knit, pass over*

╱ *Knit 2 together*

patterns — cartagena de indias

START KNITTING

FRONT

Cast on 76 [82, 90, 98] stitches.
Work rows 1–6 in Garter stitch (see page 35).
Rows 7–114 [114, 120, 124]: Work as shown in the chart.
Row 115 [115, 121, 125]: Work 14 [16, 16, 17] stitches as they appear, bind off 24 [26, 30, 32] stitches, work the rest of the stitches as they appear. Place the first 14 [16, 16, 17] stitches on hold.
Row 116 [116, 122, 126] and all even rows: Work the stitches as they appear.
Row 117 [117, 123, 127]: Bind off 3 stitches, knit 3 [5, 5, 6], work the rest of the stitches as they appear. You will have a total of 11 [13, 13, 14] stitches.
Row 119 [119, 125, 129]: Bind off 2 stitches, knit 1 [3, 3, 4], work the rest of the stitches as they appear. You will have a total of 9 [11, 11, 12] stitches.
Row 121 [121, 127, 131]: Bind off 1 stitch, knit 0 [2, 2, 3], work the rest of the stitches as they appear. You will have a total of 8 [10, 10, 11] stitches.
Row 123 [123, 129, 133] and all remaining odd rows: Knit 1 [3, 3, 4], work the rest of the stitches as they appear.

Bind off 8 [10, 10, 11] stitches.
Transfer the 14 [16, 16, 17] held stitches to a needle.
Row 116 [116, 122, 126]: Bind off 3 stitches, purl 3 [5, 5, 6], work the rest of the stitches as they appear. You will have a total of 11 [13, 13, 14] stitches.
Row 117 [117, 123, 127] and all odd rows: Work the stitches as they appear.
Row 118 [118, 124, 128]: Bind off 2 stitches, purl 1 [3, 3, 4], work the rest of the stitches as they appear. You will have a total of 9 [11, 11, 12] stitches.
Row 120 [120, 126, 130]: Bind off 1 stitch, purl 0 [2, 2, 3], work the rest of the stitches as they appear. You will have a total of 8 [10, 10, 11] stitches.
Row 122 [122, 128, 132] and remaining even rows: Purl 1 [3, 3, 4], work the rest of the stitches as they appear.
Bind off all stitches.

BACK

Cast on and work first 6 rows as for Front.
Work rows 7–118 [118, 124, 128] as shown in the chart.
Row 119 [119, 125, 129]: Work 14 [16, 16, 17] stitches as they appear, bind off 24 [26, 30, 32] stitches, work the rest of the stitches as they appear.
Place the first 14 [16, 16, 17] stitches on hold.
Row 120 [120, 126, 130] and all even rows: Work the stitches as they appear.
Row 121 [121, 127, 131]: Bind off 3 stitches, knit 3 [5, 5, 6], work the rest of the stitches as they appear. You will have a total of 11 [13, 13, 14] stitches.
Row 123 [123, 129, 133]: Bind off 2 stitches, knit 1 [3, 3, 4], work the rest of the stitches as they appear. You will have a total of 9 [11, 11, 12] stitches.
Row 125 [125, 131, 135]: Bind off 1 stitch, knit 0 [2, 2, 3], work the rest of the stitches as they appear. You will have a total of 8 [10, 10, 11] stitches.
Bind off 8 [10, 10, 11] stitches.
Transfer the 14 [16, 16, 17] held stitches to a needle.
Row 120 [120, 126, 130]: Bind off 3 stitches, purl 3 [5, 5, 6], work the rest of the stitches as they appear.

You will have a total of 11 [13, 13, 14] stitches.

Row 121 [121, 127, 131] and all odd rows: Work the stitches as they appear.

Row 122 [122, 128, 132]: Bind off 2 stitches, purl 1 [3, 3, 4], work the rest of the stitches as they appear. You will have a total of 9 [11, 11, 12] stitches.

Row 124 [124, 130, 134]: Bind off 1 stitch, purl 0 [2, 2, 3], work the rest of the stitches as they appear. You will have a total of 8 [10, 10, 11] stitches.

Row 126 [126, 132, 136]: Purl 1 [3, 3, 4], work the rest of the stitches as they appear. Bind off all stitches.

FINISHING

1.
Thread the tapestry needle with the same yarn that you used for your project and sew one of the shoulders: Place the front and back with the wrong sides together, lining up the shoulder seams. Sew 8 [10, 10, 11] stitches from one of the shoulders.

2.
Pick up and knit 100 [104, 112, 116] stitches around the neck (54 [56, 60, 62] from the front and 46 [48, 52, 54] from the back). Bind off all picked-up stitches.

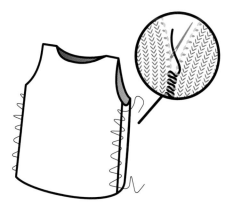

3.
Sew the ends of the neck seam and the second shoulder seam.
Sew the side seams with a zigzag stitch.

4.
Weave in all ends.

Ciudad de México

WHERE TO KNIT
Maque: Located in the beautiful area of Condesa, this ancient cafeteria is a must-visit if you are ever in town. Its *conchas* are to die for.

Parque Lincoln: Beautiful park in the middle of the fancy Polanco neighborhood.

Laguna de Chapultepec: The biggest park in the city, it is always full of people and food trucks with local sweets. There is a big lake and a castle on top of the hill where you can see the whole city. Perfect to escape from the noise of CDMX.

AVERAGE HIGH TEMPERATURES
Spring: 79.3°F (26.3°C)
Summer: 75.4°F (24.1°C)
Fall: 73.0°F (22.8°C)
Winter: 71.8°F (22.1°C)

RAINY SEASON
July and August

FAVORITE DISHES
Chilaquiles
Tacos
Frijoles

VEGGIE OPTIONS
Quesadillas
Nopales

we are knitters

Papel picado, *bordados otomíes*, Frida Kahlo, *calacas* . . . these are just a few of the Mexican arts and artists that have influenced makers, designers, and fashion around the world. Because especially in Mexico, it's all about color!

With relatives living in Mexico, we've been exposed to these super bright, happy, and vibrant colors for years. Oh, and the ways to mix them! Their uses of color have inspired us in very BIG ways when choosing the different shades of our yarns. All we have to say is, *¡Gracias México!*

Ciudad de México has a very stable temperature year-round. Some call it the City of the Never-Ending Spring. It is sunny and warm during the day, but at night it can get chilly. So before you ask yourself if knitwear is needed in a city like CDMX, the answer is yes. In fact, historically Mexican people used to wear ponchos and *rebozos* made of cotton, wool, or silk. And while most people don't wear ponchos anymore, *rebozos* are still heavily used by indigenous women to carry babies or heavy things on their backs.

In this section you will find two very simple patterns: a cowl and a blanket, both of which are made all the more beautiful with bold, bright colors, like they would make in Mexico. *¡Que les vaya bonito, amigos!*

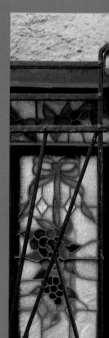

Downtown Snood

LEVEL
Beginner

FINISHED MEASUREMENTS
11" (28 cm) wide x 23½" (60 cm) circumference

YARN
We Are Knitters The Wool [100% Peruvian wool; 87 yards (80 meters)/200 grams]:
1 ball Aquamarine

NEEDLES
One pair straight needles size US 19 (15 mm)
Change needle size if necessary to obtain correct gauge.

NOTIONS
Tapestry needle

GAUGE
6 sts and 9 rows = 4" (10 cm) in Seed stitch (see page 40)

● Stitches
○ Rows

SCHEMATICS

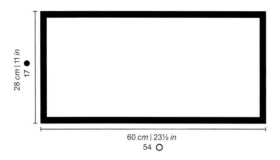

28 cm | 11 in
17

60 cm | 23½ in
54 ○

START KNITTING

Cast on 17 stitches.
Rows 1–54: Slip 1, *knit 1, purl 1*; repeat from * to * to end for Seed stitch.
Bind off all stitches.

FINISHING

Thread the tapestry needle with the same yarn used for your project and sew the ends together, with right sides facing out, with a zigzag stitch, picking up one stitch from each end of the snood.
Weave in all ends.

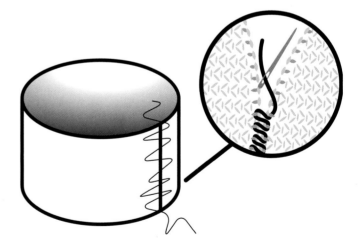

we are knitters

patterns — ciudad de méxico

No. 3 Blanket

LEVEL
Easy

FINISHED MEASUREMENTS
28" (71 cm) wide x
56" (143 cm) long

YARN
We Are Knitters The
Petite Wool [100%
Peruvian wool; 153 yards
(140 meters)/100 grams]:
6 balls Natural

NEEDLES
One 24" (60 cm)

circular needle size US
11 (8 mm)
Change needle size
if necessary to obtain
correct gauge.

NOTIONS
Tapestry needle

GAUGE
12 sts and 20 rows =
4" (10 cm) in Seed stitch
(see page 40)

● *Stitches*
○ *Rows*

SCHEMATICS

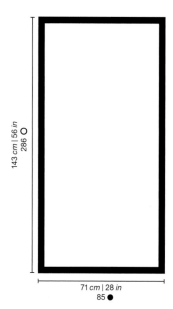

143 cm | 56 in
286 ○

71 cm | 28 in
85 ●

START KNITTING

Cast on 85 stitches.
Rows 1–286: *Knit 1, purl 1*; repeat
from * to * to end for Seed stitch.
Bind off all stitches.

FINISHING

Weave in all ends.

we are knitters

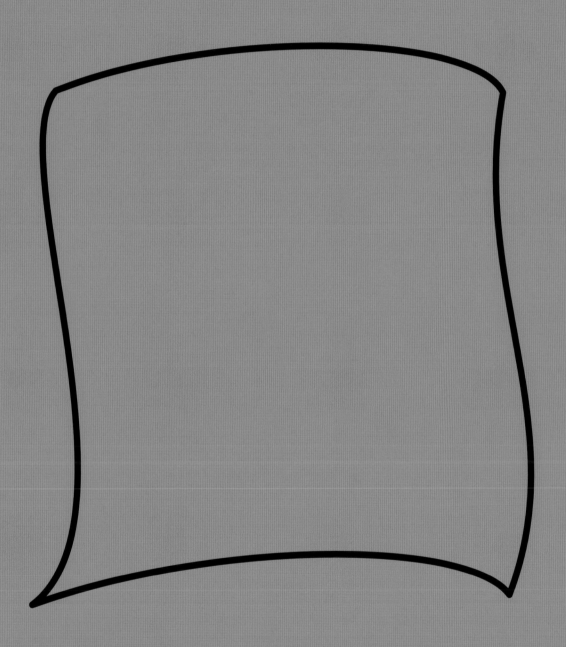

Community

When we first started, in spite of its popularity, knitting was still talked about as something that only grandmas did (nothing against grandmas!), not young people. As a result, when we thought about naming the company, we wanted to make everyone (young and old) feel that they were a part of something. That's how the name "We Are Knitters" originated.

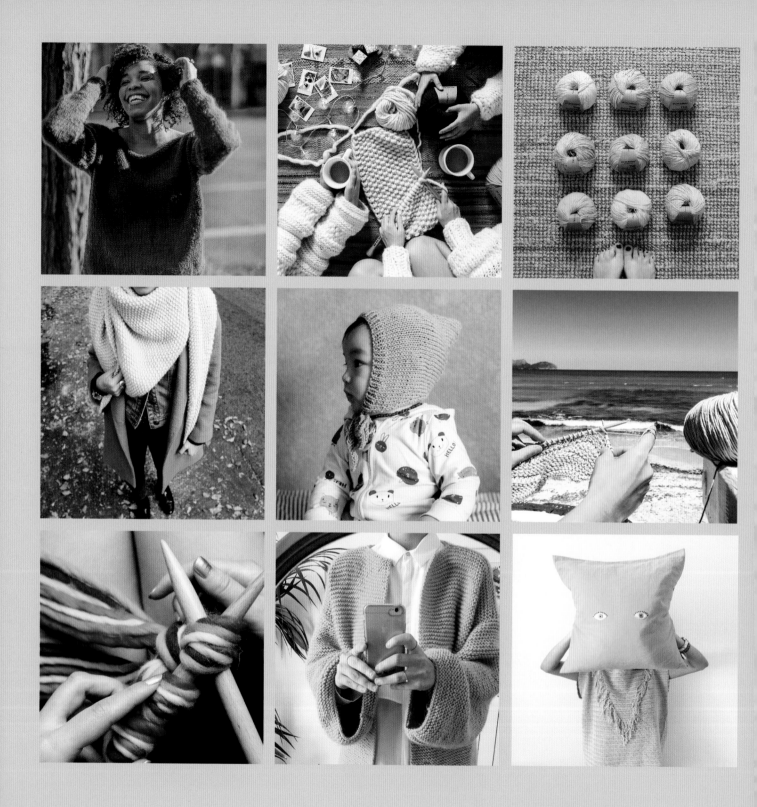

we are knitters

During WAK's early stages, social media was exploding. People were using Facebook and Twitter more and more, and Instagram was just starting to become popular. Because we were active users of these platforms, it was natural that the WAK brand would join them, too. Once it did, we couldn't believe how willing knitters were to share their achievements, FOR REAL.

We think the reason behind this impulse to share is because we live in the twenty-first century, where we spend so much of our time in front of a screen: on a laptop at work, on our phones on the street, watching TV at home—we hardly use our hands to even write anymore! It feels a little as though we have forgotten how to use our hands to make things. To combat this, makers everywhere are turning to knitting and cooking and weaving and painting. When we make something with our hands, we feel proud and we want to share it with others. And so, as contradictory as it may sound, we turn to a platform on social media to tell the world all about what we've made. It's just a sign of the times, isn't it?

Once we joined social media as WAK, we noticed a mini community started to grow. Knitters were sharing the whole experience: the moment the package was delivered (some people even included the delivery man in their pics!), the packaging, and, of course, the needles, yarn, and patterns. You could see how they were progressing with their projects and there were so many #OOTD (outfits of the day) and #weareknitters pics we just couldn't keep up!

Today we have a huge community on every social media platform. We love to share content created by our knitters to show everyone that they can do it, too. And this book offers a new way to join the WAK community and engage with other great makers just like you. #weareknitters

Resources

Commit with a Kit

When you think about WAK, a big, chunky skein of wool in a flashy color is sure to come to mind—probably with a pair of wooden needles, too—and so, by extension, do our kits.

When we first started to knit by ourselves, we realized how lost we were: We didn't know what kind of yarn to use, the size of the needles, if the pattern we wanted to make would turn out OK, etc. Yup, we were completely lost. That's why we decided that a kit containing all the materials needed to make a project would be like a dream come true.

The biggest advantage of a kit is convenience. Just choose the project you would like to make in your favorite color and skill level, and you will receive a beautiful and recyclable package with everything you need to make your project. These kits also contain easy-to-follow patterns, a small tapestry needle to weave in the ends, and a WAK tag. All the happiness that comes from knitting is right there in that kit.

Even More Resources

Keep in mind that you can always purchase individual items to fulfill all your knitting needs from WAK, too: We have skeins in every color and needles in every size. We also have a YouTube channel with tons of tutorial videos, with even more techniques explained in the same step-by-step way that we used here in this book.

And always be sure to check out and support your local yarn and craft stores for additional items. We're one big community of makers, and a little support goes a long way. Like we said before, makers gonna make!

About We Are Knitters

We wish we could tell a romantic story about our grandmothers teaching us how to knit in front of a fireplace, but the truth is that we learned how to knit watching video tutorials on the Internet. And, slowly we started to like it. OK—we LOVED it! We could make a scarf! With our own hands! And it looked good! Well, maybe a few stitches didn't look that good, and its shape was not that even, but as a whole it looked nice (or, at least, it did to us).

we are knitters

And it was super satisfying to be able to do something creative while having fun. So we kept practicing, slowly improving, and we kept watching tutorials.

It was in these moments that an idea came up: What if we made knitting super cool? We figured, if we could learn how to knit without ever having touched a pair of needles before, why wouldn't other people be able to do the same?

We launched our website in late summer 2011 without knowing what to expect. Would people like the idea of the kit we had come up with? Was the wool good enough? Were the colors beautiful? Were the patterns written correctly? So. Many. Questions.

Thanks in large part to the huge growth social media experienced at that time, we were able to reach a lot of people. Our first customers (or knitters) were based in large cities like Barcelona, Paris, and Berlin, but soon we started to receive orders from smaller towns we had never heard of before. How was this happening?

And while we don't want to bore you with too many more details, We Are Knitters has now reached more than 200,000 people across the globe. From the United States to France, Germany to Australia, Chile to Japan, and, honestly, almost everywhere in between.

We are proud that after all this time our brand has maintained those initial beliefs and feelings that allowed us to reach such a wide audience: respect for the environment and love for anything handmade. And that still today, no matter where you are, where you're going, or what you want to make, you can still get all the happiness you need in a kit.

About the Authors

So who are we? Our names are Pepita Marín and Alberto Bravo, and together we founded We Are Knitters back in 2011. We met around 2009 in Madrid, when we were both working for a consulting company. Yep, you read that correctly: We used to have completely different lives than the ones we have now. No creativity at all! When we met, we became friends immediately and realized that those jobs were not for us. We both had always wanted to be entrepreneurs and both of us loved fashion. After a trip to New York the following year, we came up with the idea of WAK, and a few years later here we are!

When we first started it was only the two of us. Now we are thirty people in our headquarters. Yup, you're right—that's a lot of coffee being served at the office in the mornings. There are people from different nationalities and cultures, a fact that we really enjoy. Some people call us the UN of knitting, and they're kinda right. You walk through our office and you hear people speaking in English, Spanish, French, German, etc. This is one of the reasons why we have the whole website and all the patterns available in more than ten different languages and counting!

At the very beginning, we only used to launch a couple of collections a year. Can you imagine? Who did we think we were? Coco Chanel? Now we launch new patterns on an almost weekly basis. We realized that we makers need new projects almost constantly. When you're almost done with your current project, you're already thinking about the next one. There are collections for every taste: knitting, crochet, petit point, style-themed collections, stitch-themed collections, etc. There are more than five hundred different kits available now in our online store. That's A LOT of stitches to make, if you ask us. And we wouldn't have it any other way.

Acknowledgments

We would like to take this opportunity to thank all the people who have helped us along the way. There are a lot of you, so we cannot name you all (we don't want to forget anyone), but we're sure you know who you are! First and foremost, to our families, who have supported us through thick and thin. Your help was key at the very beginning, when no one believed in our idea. Without you it wouldn't have been the same.

To our friends! Some of you came with us to trade shows, assembled (a lot) of kits at the very beginning, posed for our photo shoots, and even knitted pieces for us! You are a treasure to us!

To the whole We Are Knitters team—YOU ROCK!! We're so thankful to be surrounded by so many talented people. If WAK is anything today, it is because of you and your passion and hard work. All of you. We would especially like to thank Raquel Porter, Monica Ceballos, Lorena Fernández, Ana de Luis, Erika Beltrán, Victor Seco, Chloé Ricaud, and Francesca Maiorino. Your creativity and vision are in these pages.

To the old and new friends we made while shooting these photos: Thank you for being so patient while on vacation and giving us your time so generously, especially Virginia Sánchez, Paula Alonso, Aston Albiach, Iván Ovejero, Blanca Bravo, Udayan Mazumbar, Mariana Tello, Israel Alvarez, Miriam Martín, Paula Tébar, Jewel Washington, and Mindy Diaz. :)

To our editor, Meredith Clark. You've been so helpful and supportive along the process. Thank you for letting us make what we had

in mind into a reality and guiding us with your experience. This book is yours, too!

And last but not least, to all the makers around the globe: You are all da bomb! We will be thankful for your support until the end of time. And don't forget that makers make the world go 'round (one stitch at a time)!

EDITOR
Meredith A. Clark

DESIGNER
Sebit Min

PRODUCTION MANAGER
Rebecca Westall

Library of Congress Control
Number: 2018958255

ISBN: 978-1-4197-3612-4
eISBN: 978-1-68335-670-7
Text and photography copyright
© 2019 We Are Knitters

Cover © 2019 Abrams

Printed and bound in China
10 9 8 7 6 5 4 3 2 1

Abrams books are available at special discounts when purchased in
quantity for premiums and promo-
tions as well as fundraising or edu-
cational use. Special editions can
also be created to specification.
For details, contact specialsales@
abramsbooks.com or the address
below.

Abrams® is a registered trademark
of Harry N. Abrams, Inc.

ABRAMS
The Art of Books

195 Broadway
New York, NY 10007
abramsbooks.com